C000235340

To:
_____

From:
_____

Message:
_____
_____
_____

Published by Christian Art Publishers
PO Box 1599, Vereeniging, 1930, RSA

© 2022
First edition 2022

Designed by Christian Art Publishers
Devotions taken from *Every Day with God* by Cherie Hill

Cover designed by Christian Art Publishers
Images used under license from Shutterstock.com

Unless otherwise indicated, Scripture quotations are taken from
the Holy Bible, New Living Translation, copyright © 1996, 2004, 2015
by Tyndale House Foundation. Used by permission of Tyndale House
Publishers, Carol Stream, Illinois 60188. All rights reserved.

Scripture quotations marked GW are taken from the GOD'S WORD
Translation (GW). Copyright © 1995 by God's Word to the Nations.
Used by permission of Baker Publishing Group.

Scripture quotations marked NIV are taken from the Holy Bible,
New International Version®, NIV® Copyright © 1973, 1978, 1984, 2011
by Biblica, Inc.® Used by permission. All rights reserved worldwide.

Scripture quotations marked ESV are taken from the Holy Bible,
English Standard Version®. ESV® Text Edition: 2016. Copyright © 2001
by Crossway, a publishing ministry of Good News Publishers.
Used by permission. All rights reserved.

Scripture quotations marked AMP are taken from the Amplified® Bible
(AMP), Copyright © 2015 by The Lockman Foundation.
Used by permission. www.Lockman.org

Printed in China

ISBN 978-1-77637-175-4

© All rights reserved. No part of this book may be reproduced in any
form without permission in writing from the publisher, except in the
case of brief quotations in critical articles or reviews.

23 24 25 26 27 28 29 30 31 32 – 12 11 10 9 8 7 6 5 4 3

Printed in Shenzhen, China
SEPTEMBER 2023
Print Run: PUR403313

MINI DEVOTIONS for KIDS

CHERIE HILL

CHRISTIAN ART PUBLISHERS

Count Them

All praise to God, the Father of our Lord Jesus Christ,
who has blessed us with every spiritual blessing in
the heavenly realms because we are united with Christ.
EPHESIANS 1:3

I want you to always be thankful for what you have and realize that I AM always looking for ways to bless you.

While you're waiting for Me to answer prayers, I want you to look for ways that you can be a blessing to others. Every time I bless you, I AM giving you a little bit of heaven on earth. You can be a blessing to others and bring them a little heaven too.

Lord, help me to be a blessing to others and
trust that You will take care of all of my needs. Amen.

What You Really Need

You don't have what you want
because you don't ask God for it.
JAMES 4:2

Sometimes you worry, get upset, and get frustrated that things aren't working out in your life, and sometimes that's because you haven't asked Me for what you want or need.

Even though I already know your wants and needs, getting closer to Me and knowing Me better means talking to Me and asking Me for things. Doing this makes your faith stronger and that's what you really need.

Heavenly Father, when I'm worried
and upset, remind me to come to You
and ask for what I need. Amen.

The Free Gift

The promise is received by faith.
It is given as a free gift.
ROMANS 4:16

There's really not much in your life that you will ever get for free, but My love for you and My promises to you are free … when you believe in Me and My Son, Jesus. There is nothing you have to do to earn My love and My promises. That is a blessing you can be thankful for.

When you feel empty, like nothing is going your way, I want you to stop and think about all of the good things in your life that I have given to you and realize that you should be thankful because they are free gifts.

Lord, thank You for Your promises.
Thank You for being with me
and giving me hope. Amen.

Hidden Blessings

"Don't be afraid, for I am with you. Don't be discouraged,
for I am your God. I will strengthen you and help you.
I will hold you up with My victorious right hand."
ISAIAH 41:10

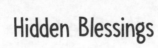

When life is hard, I know it seems like it's all My fault and
you don't think I know what I'm doing. But sometimes I
allow things to be hard so it gives your faith a chance to
grow. When you have troubles, they are hidden blessings
because they give you a chance to believe in Me more.

So, when troubles come, stop and remember that I've
promised to work all things together for good.

Dear God, I know that sometimes I am not
thankful when life is hard … help me to
see that You are giving me stronger faith
when there is trouble in my life. Amen.

Trust Me

The LORD is good to those whose hope
is in Him, to the one who seeks Him.
LAMENTATIONS 3:25 (NIV)

When you're down and alone and sad, I want you to count your blessings—focus on all of the good things in your life. When life is hard, it's really easy to lose hope, so I want you to keep thinking about My promises.

Even when it seems like there is no hope, I want you to trust Me and remember that I can do the impossible. There is always hope if you will pray to Me and keep looking for Me to answer your prayers.

Heavenly Father, help me to count my blessings
and be thankful for the small things in
my life as well as the big things. Amen.

I Am with You

Yet, I am always with You. You hold on to
my right hand. With Your advice You guide me,
and in the end You will take me to glory.
PSALM 73:23-24 (GW)

You might not know where your life is headed. Things might seem confusing, but I know your life from beginning to end and I know every decision you need to make to go down the right path.

When life is hard and confusing, you need to know that I AM always with you, so that you don't have to be afraid. Just like if we were walking in the park, I AM holding your hand, walking through life.

Heavenly Father, I find peace in knowing
that You are in control of my life and that
You love me. Help me to do what is right,
so that I can live a life of blessing. Amen.

Walk with Me

We can make our plans,
but the Lᴏʀᴅ determines our steps.
PROVERBS 16:9

I know that you like to make plans for your life, you have ideas of what you want to be and what you want to do, but I want you to know that My plans for your life are way bigger and better.

So, I don't want you to try and live each day on your own. I want you to always pray to Me so that I can help you make right decisions that will lead you down the right path that I have planned for you. I'll guide you … step by step.

Lord, I look to You to lead
and guide me step by step
so that I will follow
Your good plan for my life. Amen.

Follow My Path

He renews my strength. He guides me
along right paths, bringing honor to His name.
PSALM 23:3

Sometimes life will be very confusing and it will be hard
to know which way to go. But remember I AM always with
you. I will always help you to see which way is the right
way—sometimes My Spirit will speak to your heart and you
will just know what to do. Other times, you will need to
read the Bible and listen for My voice in your heart.

I know the ways I lead you might not always be easy,
but they are the right ways—they are My ways.

Dear God, help me to be strong even when
the way You lead me in life might be hard.
Help me to praise You as I walk with You. Amen.

Trust in My Plans

"I know the plans I have for you ..."
JEREMIAH 29:11

When your day doesn't go as planned, try not to stop believing or praying to Me. When your life seems out of control, you need to know it's still in My control.

Even though sometimes My plans might seem too hard or like they're not leading you in the right direction, I want you to be sure that My plans are always what is best for you. And even though things might be tough, I AM with you to help you. And in the end, everything is going to work out—you don't need to worry.

Lord, help me to trust You when I'm confused and want to go my own way in life. Help me to trust in Your plans and know that You love me and will always do what is best for me. Amen.

I Will Figure It Out

The LORD directs our steps, so why try
to understand everything along the way?
PROVERBS 20:24

I don't want you to always try to understand everything in your life—because you won't. I have amazing plans for your life, and they are for good, but you won't always understand.

I want you to learn to let go, to be at peace, and know that I will always strengthen you to have the faith you need to keep trusting Me to help you with each step of your life. Trust Me to do the impossible and know that I will always do what is best for you.

Heavenly Father, help me to let go and
let You handle all of the detail of my life
so that I don't have to worry. Amen.

Pray for Help

"Don't worry about tomorrow, for tomorrow will bring
its own worries. Today's trouble is enough for today."
MATTHEW 6:34

I do not want you wasting your time worrying about
tomorrow—you've got more than enough problems to
deal with today. So, I want you to focus on and pray
about "today", not tomorrow.

There are so many things in life that you can't control.
I want you to stay focused on Me and My power and all I
can do to help you. I can do the impossible.

Heavenly Father, help me to focus on today
and not worry about tomorrow. Amen.

Guarded by Angels

He will put His angels in charge of you
to protect you in all your ways.
PSALM 91:11 (GW)

I AM always watching over you and you should know that My angels are watching over you too—all the time. So, I don't want you to worry, I want you to be at peace.

I want you to learn to have faith and to trust Me even when things seem really bad. When you're afraid and feeling all alone, I want you to come to Me in prayer and ask for My help. Then, wait patiently, knowing that I AM always loving you and protecting you.

Lord God, thank You for Your angels that are always watching over me so that I can be at peace. Amen.

I AM at Work in You

Because of His glory and excellence, He has given us
great and precious promises. These are the promises
that enable you to share His divine nature and escape
the world's corruption caused by human desires.

2 PETER 1:4

I have made so many promises for your life—big and small, and I want you to know them all.

When you are afraid of the future, upset and worried, I want you to know I AM with you—right where you are. I AM always looking for ways to bless you, always at work, doing what is best for your life. But don't try to understand everything I AM doing, because you can't. Just trust that I AM in control and everything is going to be okay.

Dear God, I am so thankful for the promises
You've made me so that I can have hope and
trust You even when I don't understand. Amen.

I Will Provide

He has shown kindness by giving you rain
from heaven and crops in their seasons; He provides
you with plenty of food and fills your hearts with joy.
ACTS 14:17 (NIV)

I know sometimes you worry if you will have "enough". Enough friends, enough "things", but you need to remember that I have promised that you will always have enough. I know exactly what you need.

I promise you that My plans for your life are far better than anything you might have planned. So, I want you to learn to trust Me and be at peace that whatever you need I will give you.

Lord God, help me to be satisfied with
what I have and know that You will always
make sure I have "enough". Amen.

Trust Me for Miracles

Then Moses stretched out his hand over the sea, and the
LORD drove the sea back by a strong east wind all night
and made the sea dry land, and the waters were divided.
EXODUS 14:21 (ESV)

Maybe you've read or heard when I split open the seas
so that I could help people from evil and danger ... it's
the story of the Red Sea being parted. I want you to
know about this because it shows you how powerful I
AM, and how I can make miracles happen, even at the
last minute.

So, just because things seem really bad and it doesn't
look like things are going to get better, it doesn't mean
that it will stay that way. I can do ANYTHING in the blink
of an eye.

Heavenly Father, thank You for the Bible that
teaches me about Your love and power and
that You can do the impossible. Amen.

Shine My Light

Since God chose you to be the holy people He loves,
you must clothe yourselves with tenderhearted mercy,
kindness, humility, gentleness, and patience.
COLOSSIANS 3:12

I know sometimes life is confusing and you're not really sure what you're supposed to be doing, but there is always one thing that I want you to remember to do—be a light to those living in this dark world.

Others need to know Jesus too, and you can lead them to Him by being loving and kind. So, when you're not sure what to do with your faith, know that you can always be a bright shining light.

Heavenly Father, help me to be a light
to others and lead them to You so they will
know Your amazing love and grace. Amen.

Live Your Faith

My message and my preaching were very plain.
Rather than using clever and persuasive speeches,
I relied only on the power of the Holy Spirit.
1 CORINTHIANS 2:4

Because you have faith in Me it does not mean that I want you to go around preaching all of the time. Others will see your faith in Me by what you say and do.

So, I want you to pray that the Holy Spirit will work in you and help you to pray for others and lead them to Me by just being who I've created you to be. If you'll just allow Me to work through you to reach others, you'll find yourself bringing a little heaven to earth.

Lord, open my eyes to the needs of others and
to pray for them to come to You so that they
might receive Your grace when they need it. Amen.

Cling to Your Faith

As for you, be strong and do not give up,
for your work will be rewarded.
2 CHRONICLES 15:7 (NIV)

I know that sometimes faith is really hard. You try really hard to say and do the right things, but you're not sure if you're doing things well.

I want you to know that My Spirit will always help you. You don't need to try and do everything on your own. I will always lead and guide you and help you to know what to do. When you're weak, I will carry you and if you do not give up, I will reward you.

Dear God, help me to be strong and not give up in
my faith, even when life is really hard. Please lead
and guide me when I don't know what to do. Amen.

Serve with Strength

Whoever speaks must speak God's words.
Whoever serves must serve with the strength
God supplies so that in every way God receives
glory through Jesus Christ. Glory and power
belong to Jesus Christ forever and ever! Amen.

1 PETER 4:11 (GW)

You were put on the earth for big reasons. The most important reason is to help others learn about Me. When you look for ways to help others, when you are kind and giving, you are helping others to see Me.

Each and every day, even when things are not going just right in your life, I want you to be strong and serve others by paying attention to their needs. I want you to always believe what I've promised to you—I will give you all you need and more.

Heavenly Father, help me to be strong
and speak Your words, even when it feels
uncomfortable. Open my eyes to helping others
around me to see who You are. Amen.

I Chose You

"Go! I've chosen this man to bring My name
to nations, to kings, and to the people."
ACTS 9:15 (GW)

I know that sometimes you feel like you don't have what it takes to help others to see Jesus. But if you will just pray to Me for help, My Spirit will do all the work.

I will fill you with wisdom that tells you what to do and I will give you love in your heart to do what must be done. It might be helping a friend or being kind to someone who has no friends. But don't be afraid ... I have chosen you and I will help you.

Lord God, thank You for choosing me to help
You love others. Give me the strength
and faith to do what You want me to do. Amen.

Look to Me for Joy

When he arrived and saw what the grace of God
had done, he was glad and encouraged them all
to remain true to the Lord with all their hearts.

ACTS 11:23 (NIV)

It's okay to feel sad. There will be things in life that make you feel alone and like life is just not fair. I AM here for you when things aren't going right and you're not sure if things are going to get better.

I want you to have joy every day. Even on the days when you don't feel full of joy, you can still have joy because I AM God and I will give you hope.

Lord God, help me to have joy every day,
even though sometimes I don't feel joyful.
Help me to look to You for my joy. Amen.

Wait On Me

O Lord my God, You have performed many wonders
for us. Your plans for us are too numerous to list.
You have no equal. If I tried to recite all Your wonderful
deeds, I would never come to the end of them.

PSALM 40:5

When you're feeling sad, I want you to remember that not only have I promised to always be with you, but I've promised to give you a future and a hope.

You should know that I spend time thinking about you. I know all of the things that make you sad. It's not always easy to wait on Me to answer your prayers, especially when you're really sad. Keep praying and keep being glad that I will do wonderful things in your life.

Heavenly Father, help me to always trust You, to wait
on You, and to know that You can do miracles. Amen.

Hold On to Me

The LORD lives! Thanks be to my rock!
May God, the rock of my salvation, be glorified.
2 SAMUEL 22:47 (GW)

There are always going to be a lot of things that change in your life and I know that life is hard when things change. But I want you to be still and be strong ... I will give you strength. Just keep believing in the promises I've made you.

I will help you to be calm. I just need you to be thankful for all I've done for you and look forward to all that I will still do. No matter how crazy life is ... I AM your Rock.

Lord God, thank You for being my Rock,
keeping me calm and at peace, knowing that
You will always help me and protect me,
and give me joy in knowing You. Amen.

Never Give Up

Since we are surrounded by so many examples
of faith, we must get rid of everything that slows
us down, especially sin that distracts us. We must
run the race that lies ahead of us and never give up.
HEBREWS 12:1 (GW)

When you look around, you will see things that make you sad and even mad, but when you look up, you'll see Me. I AM always with you, when nothing is going right, when you're feeling worried and not sure that you believe in Me anymore.

Just choose to be glad, choose not to be sad, keep praying and never give up.

Dear God, remind my heart that all I need to do is
pray and not give up. Help me to trust that You are
with me and I should not be afraid or worry. Amen.

I AM All You Need

The LORD is my shepherd;
I have all that I need.
PSALM 23:1

You may think you need a lot of things, but all you really need is Me. Don't get too worried about what you do or don't have. Just be thankful and glad for today—for right now.

There is no reason to worry ... there's no reason to be upset or sad. Like a shepherd that leads and cares for his sheep, I will lead you ... showing you what you should do. I will care for you in every way, so you don't have to worry. I will give you all you need.

Lord God, I sometimes feel like I need more,
like I don't have enough. Turn my heart
and eyes to You ... to remember that I
have all that I need if I have You. Amen.

Help in Trouble

God is our refuge and strength,
always ready to help in times of trouble.
PSALM 46:1

There will always be troubles in your life—some that you create, and some that you don't. I AM with you through them all. When life gets too hard, I know it can make you question if I'm real and if I really care about you. But just because life doesn't make sense, doesn't mean you should stop believing.

You must keep believing, no matter what. The ways I answer your prayers and help you can happen suddenly, or take time. So, I need you to be patient, keep praying and know that I will help you.

Father in heaven, I need to trust You more.
When I am in trouble, I need Your strength.
Help me to know You are always with me. Amen.

Keep Believing

We are hard pressed on every side,
but not crushed; perplexed, but not
in despair; persecuted, but not abandoned;
struck down, but not destroyed.
2 CORINTHIANS 4:8-9 (NIV)

Sometimes it might seem like life is just too hard. You might feel like I'm not fair and that I don't care. But I've promised you that no matter how things look, I AM always working everything together for good.

Don't be afraid when you have problems in your life. Your problems give you a chance to come to Me, pray and get closer to Me, and allow Me to show you the miracles I can do in your life. Keep your eyes on Me and keep believing.

Lord God, I feel like so many things in my life
are not going right. I don't know what to do
and I need Your help so that I don't lose hope
in Your promise that things will get better. Amen.

Hard Times Don't Last

"In this world you will have trouble.
But take heart! I have overcome the world."
JOHN 16:33 (NIV)

I know there comes a time when life is just too hard and you need it all to stop. Just know that sometimes I allow problems in your life to draw you nearer to Me, to make you trust Me more—to make your faith stronger.

When you are frustrated, I want you to come to Me, thanking Me for all of the good things in your life—be thankful—even when life is hard. These hard times won't last, I've promised you that I will end them, just trust Me and be at peace.

Father in heaven, I am going through
a really hard time right now and I need
Your help. Help me to trust in You and
know that things will get better soon. Amen.

I AM Close to You

Why, Lord, do You stand far off?
Why do You hide Yourself in times of trouble?
PSALM 10:1 (NIV)

You might feel as though you are alone and in the dark, but I AM your light. Your faith grows when you have to trust Me during hard times and you have problems that are bigger than you.

Though you can't see Me, I AM with you always. Don't trust your feelings, only trust Me and all that I've promised you. There is nothing in your life that I can't fix. I make all things new. Right now, when you're afraid, I AM closer to you than I've ever been.

Heavenly Father, I feel so alone. I know that
I need to trust in You, but it is hard when the
things in my life are not going right. Give me peace
to know that You are always with me. Amen.

Call On Me

"When they call on Me, I will answer; I will be
with them in trouble. I will rescue and honor them."
PSALM 91:15

There is nothing for you to be afraid of—I AM bigger than anything. Your troubles might be too big for you, but nothing is too big for Me—and I AM with you always.

I will protect you and care for you and I will always be there to help you. Don't stop believing just because things don't change right away. I AM always with you to help you. I want what is best for your life—to give you good things. Just call on Me, know that I will answer, I will help you in times of trouble.

Dear God, I need help believing that You always
hear me, that You are always with me and that You
will always help me when I'm in trouble. Amen.

Look to Me

I pray that God, the source of hope,
will fill you completely with joy and peace
because you trust in Him. Then you
will overflow with confident hope
through the power of the Holy Spirit.
ROMANS 15:13

When life is hard ... when things aren't going your way and you feel frustrated, know that I have a plan to give you hope. When you feel like you cannot trust anyone else, trust Me and the promises I have made you.

Above all else you are My child and I have promised you good things for your future. When you're down, look up ... I AM with you always—hope in Me is all you need.

Lord God, help me to hope in You. Fill my heart
with Your love and help me to have peace
when life seems too hard for me. Amen.

Focus On Me

Put your hope in the Lord.
PSALM 37:34

Life is not always going to go the way you want it to, but know that it will always go according to My perfect plan. You won't always understand My ways, and at times you will question and doubt My love for you because things are just not going right. But I love you more than you can imagine and I only want good things for you.

I want you focusing on Me, instead of all that you think you want and need. It's during the hard times that I will draw you near to Me, I will hold you close and give you peace. I AM all you need and I will fill your heart with hope.

Heavenly Father, I feel as though all hope is gone.
Things aren't going right and I need You.
I pray that You fill me with Your peace
and teach me to hope in You alone. Amen.

Believe in Me

Whoever believes in Him
will not be put to shame.
1 PETER 2:6 (ESV)

I know that faith in Me is hard. You can't see Me and you can't hear Me in the ways you think you should. But one day, you will see Me face to face, in the way you want to. It's until then that I want you to just believe.

I will give you all you need each day if you will trust in Me for those things you desire. It may not always seem like I AM with you and you will often feel like you're alone, but you're not. I AM with you always ... I will not disappoint you ... just believe.

Heavenly Father, help me to believe in
You even though I can't see You and
hear You in the ways I want to right now.
Give me hope to seek You more. Amen.

Keep Praying

Why, my soul, are you downcast?
Why so disturbed within me? Put your hope in God,
for I will yet praise Him, my Savior and my God.
PSALM 43:5 (NIV)

You might feel helpless and things might seem hopeless, but everything is okay. I AM with you and I have the power to work miracles in your life. I can do the impossible. So, don't be sad, don't give up, keep trusting in Me and My promises for you … I will give you hope.

Hope is not gone when your hope is in Me. I hear every prayer you pray, I know all of your thoughts of fear and anger, and I know every tear you cry. Don't give up, nothing is too difficult for Me. Look to Me, keep praying to Me, and hold on to hope … no matter what.

Lord, help me to hold on to hope in You.
Help me to trust that You can do anything.
Give me peace that You are with me. Amen.

I AM in Control

"I know the plans that I have for you,
declares the LORD. They are plans for peace
and not disaster, plans to give
you a future filled with hope."
JEREMIAH 29:11 (GW)

Life might seem overwhelming, like nothing is going right and things are not going to get better, but that is not what I have promised you. I have promised to give you peace and fill you with hope in your life. You won't always be able to control the things in your life, but you need to know that I AM always in control.

The most important thing is that you listen to My Word and follow My instructions for your life. It will not always be easy, but My Spirit is within you to help you do what you think is too hard to do. Trust that I have good plans for you and keep looking to Me for all that you need ... especially hope.

Heavenly Father, I put my hope in You.
Help me to trust that You have good plans
for my life and I can rest in You. Amen.

Give It to Me

Casting all your cares [all your anxieties,
all your worries, and all your concerns, once and
for all] on Him, for He cares about you [with deepest
affection, and watches over you very carefully].
1 PETER 5:7 (AMP)

You need to know that I AM always watching over you, so you don't need to worry. I want you to trust that I will always take care of you and there is no reason for you to be upset or worry about anything.

I want you to rest, knowing that I AM always in control and I can fix all of your problems—big and small. All you must do is pray … talk to Me about what is bothering you. I will listen and help you to have peace while I work on fixing all the things you're worried about.

Lord God, I am giving You everything that makes
me worry. I want to trust You to take care of
my problems … big or small … and be at peace,
knowing You are watching over me. Amen.

Never Alone

Even though I walk through the [sunless] valley
of the shadow of death, I fear no evil, for You
are with me; Your rod [to protect] and Your staff
[to guide], they comfort and console me.
PSALM 23:4 (AMP)

I want you to know that I AM always with you. I AM always watching over you, always hearing your laughter, and always drying your tears.

I know what you want, and I know all that you need ... know that I can do anything, but I need you to trust Me and get to know Me better. I want you to rest, knowing that no matter how bad things might seem, I AM in control and can make all of the bad things turn to good.

Lord, when my life seems hard and
nothing is going right, help me not to worry,
but to trust that You can take all of the bad things
and use them for good in my life. Amen.

Hope in Me

There is surely a future hope for you,
and your hope will not be cut off.
PROVERBS 23:18 (NIV)

I know it sometimes seems like hope is gone, like nothing is ever going to go right, but I've promised to give you hope. Worrying won't make things better … but praying to Me to help you will.

You can win over your worries by hoping in Me and all that I've promised you. Know that I AM always looking over you and always taking care of you. If you are looking to Me and believing all that I've promised, you will always have hope.

Dear God, I need to know that there is
always hope, even when everything is wrong
and nothing seems to be getting better. Fill me
with Your peace, so that I do not worry. Amen.

Have Faith

God is with you in everything you do.
GENESIS 21:22 (NIV)

When you are worried, I know it makes you afraid ... which causes you to do things and say things you should not. I always want you to have faith ... no matter what. You won't always feel like having faith, so you will need to read the Bible, My Word, to give you peace, hope, and strength.

I AM with you in everything, I AM bigger than anything, do not worry—do not be afraid. Choose to have faith ... not fear.

Lord, I get worried because sometimes I feel so alone.
I want to trust You. Please give me the faith I need
to hope in You at all times and in all ways. Amen.

Think Good Thoughts

Don't worry.
PSALM 37:1

It's easy to just think about the things that are hard in life, the things that aren't going right in your life, instead of just thinking about Me. When you're not focused on Me, it causes you to think wrong thoughts, which only makes you worry more.

I want you to always be thinking of good things, always be praying, and make the decision to stop worrying. Know that I know your heart is hurting and I will wipe away every tear you cry. I want you to rest in Me and know that I will always help you ... I love you and everything is going to be okay.

Heavenly Father, help me to think of good things
and to focus on You, so that I do not worry.
I need You to give me peace and certainty
that everything is going to be okay. Amen.

Let Go

Give your burdens to the LORD,
and He will take care of you.
PSALM 55:22

When life isn't making sense, when you're confused and upset, I want you to just "let go" and let Me handle all that is bothering you. I want you to think about the things that are good—those things that make you happy.

I want you to stop when you're upset and know that I AM bigger than what is bothering you. I want you to enjoy your life and let Me deal with the hard stuff. I want you to give your troubles to Me and to just "let go."

Lord God, I am restless and I need You.
Please calm me and help me to know
that You have everything under control
and everything will be okay. Amen.

Trust in Me

"I know the plans that I have for you,
declares the LORD. They are plans for
peace and not disaster, plans to give
you a future filled with hope."
JEREMIAH 29:11 (GW)

Whether it's little things or big things, I need you to
come to Me and trust Me. There is nothing too small and
nothing too hard for Me. Though your frustrations in life
may be hard for you to handle, I can do anything. I can
fix what you can't. I do not become smaller just because
your problems become bigger.

I may allow hard times in your life, but when you trust
Me, your faith will grow and you will learn that I AM more
real than you could ever imagine. When you are weak,
I AM strong. So, thank Me for all I've done and all I'm
going to do. When you're happy and when you're sad,
know that I AM with you ... in everything.

Lord, I trust You. I am going through
a hard time and I need Your help.
Please let everything turn out okay. Amen.

Trust My Promises

When I worried about many things,
Your assuring words soothed my soul.
PSALM 94:19 (GW)

When you're feeling angry and unhappy with the way things are going in your life, I want you to trust that I AM all you need. I've made promises to you in My Word, the Bible, that you can count on.

I want to give you peace, so that you don't have to worry and so that you can enjoy your life. Don't be afraid, I AM with you and I've promised you good things. There is no reason to worry, no need to be upset ... I want you to enjoy the life I've given you, by trusting in the promises I've made to you.

Heavenly Father, I am thankful for
Your promises that comfort me when
I am struggling with my feelings. Please fill me
with Your peace when I am upset. Amen.

I AM Here

"Don't let your hearts be troubled.
Trust in God, and trust also in Me."
JOHN 14:1

When you're in trouble, I know it makes you angry and afraid. I AM here to assure you that, no matter what, I love you and I will help you through your troubles.

Sometimes you get in trouble because of something you've done ... sometimes it's because of what someone else has done, but it will be okay ... whatever it is ... I can fix anything. Keep praying to Me about all that is worrying you and know that I AM listening and I will help you in times of trouble.

Lord God, help me to come to You when I am
in trouble. Help me not to be afraid and to know
that You love me, no matter what. Fill my heart
with peace as I trust in You to help me. Amen.

Pray to Me

Don't worry about anything; instead, pray
about everything. Tell God what you need,
and thank Him for all He has done.
PHILIPPIANS 4:6

I know sometimes you don't think that I hear you when you pray to Me. But I hear everything. I hear your heart and I know everything that you're thinking and feeling.

So when you feel all alone, when you're worried about all the things in your life that aren't going right, just pray to Me ... ask Me for what you need and be thankful for all of the good things I've done in your life. Be thankful for the little things just like you are thankful for the big things. Be thankful, be grateful, and watch all the wonderful things that I will do in your life.

Heavenly Father, thank You for all of
the blessings You have given to me. Teach me
to be grateful for the good and bad things in
my life, knowing that You are always in control
and have good things planned for me. Amen.

I Will Keep You Safe

No weapon that has been made to
be used against you will succeed.
ISAIAH 54:17 (GW)

It's easy to feel like everyone and everything is against you—sometimes that might be true. But there is no reason to fear, I am with you to protect you and keep you safe and sound.

So if friends aren't nice, if you're feeling scared of things around you, remember that I have promised to stand up for you and to protect you. Nothing can get in the way of My love for you. You are always safe in My arms.

Lord God, I need to know that You will
protect me and keep me safe and sound. Amen.

I AM Your Rescuer

My eyes are always on the LORD,
for He rescues me from the traps of my enemies.
PSALM 25:15

When you are afraid, you first need to come to Me. I AM always with you to help you. My Word, the Bible, can keep you from being afraid if you trust that I've promised to love you and protect you.

I will rescue you from the bad things in life, but sometimes you must wait because My plan can take time—so I need you to have faith and believe in Me even when it's hard.

Heavenly Father, when I need You to protect Me and rescue Me, I will pray to You and trust that You are with Me and will do all that You've promised. Amen.

Guard Your Heart

The peace of God, which transcends all understanding,
will guard your hearts and your minds in Christ Jesus.
PHILIPPIANS 4:7 (NIV)

I realize that sometimes your sadness makes it feel like your heart is breaking. Know that I know about every tear that you cry. I don't want you to lose hope or give up when life is hard. I want you to come to Me and know that I will protect you and guard your heart.

Come to Me when you are sad and afraid—pray to Me—talk to Me like a friend and know that I hear you. Give Me your heart and I will guard it and comfort you—I will give you peace.

Lord, I am so sad, but I know that You
are with me. Please take my heart and keep
it safe. Comfort me with Your love. Amen.

Rest in My Shadow

Whoever dwells in the shelter of the Most High
will rest in the shadow of the Almighty.
PSALM 91:1 (NIV)

I know that when you are sad or afraid you need to know that I AM with you to protect you. And I know that since you can't see Me, it is hard to believe. That's why I've given you the Bible, My promises to you, so that you can learn to have faith and trust Me.

You should know that I've promised to shelter you and to protect you. Even if bad things happen to you, I AM always with you and will one day make all of the bad things good. Come to Me and I will shelter you—you can rest in My shadow.

Lord God, help me to rest and know that
You will be with me and protect me.
Help me to have greater faith in You. Amen.

My Shield of Love

Let all who take refuge in You rejoice.
Spread Your protection over them.
For You bless the godly, O Lord;
You surround them with Your shield of love.
PSALM 5:11-12

There will be times when life is so hard that everything will seem dark and scary and lonely, but you must remember that I AM always with you. Even when hope seems gone, it is not because it is hopeless. I can do anything ... all you must do is trust in Me.

You are my child and I will always watch over you and love you. I want you to come to Me when you're in trouble or afraid. My love is a shield for your heart, to give you peace at all times.

Dear God, help me to have peace and joy,
even when life is hard and I'm worried and afraid.
Help me to trust You more and more. Amen.

Just Ask

You don't have what you want
because you don't ask God for it.
JAMES 4:2

I always want to help you, but you need to ask for My help. I hear every prayer that you pray. I know every tear that you cry. I know when you are tired and frustrated and I can give you peace in your heart—just ask me.

I don't just care about the big things going on in your life, I care about the small things too. I AM never too busy to help you ... so come to Me, just ask for what you need.

Lord God, thank You for always hearing
my prayers. I get tired and frustrated and
I need You to help me to have peace in
my heart, knowing that You are with me. Amen.

I'll Calm Your Fears

Praise be to the God and Father of our Lord Jesus
Christ, the Father of compassion and the God of
all comfort, who comforts us in all our troubles,
so that we can comfort those in any trouble with
the comfort we ourselves receive from God.

2 CORINTHIANS 1:3-4 (NIV)

When you're upset, confused, or afraid, what do you do first? I always need you to come to Me before you do anything. Always pray to Me when you don't know what to do.

I can calm your fears, I can give your heart peace, and I will always give you hope when you're confused. Remember that I can do the impossible, so keep asking Me for miracles in your life.

Dear God, please calm my fears. Thank You
for always being there to comfort me when
I have troubles in my life and helping me
when I don't know what to do. Amen.

You're Not Forgotten

O Lᴏʀᴅ, how long will You forget me?
PSALM 13:1

I know that when life gets hard, it seems like I've forgotten about you, but I never forget about you. I AM always thinking of you—I love you and I care about everything in your life.

I want you to learn to be strong, knowing that I'm with you. I will always keep the promises that I have made to you. I do not lie. I want you to trust Me to always do what's best for you because I know your life from beginning to end.

Heavenly Father, thank You for never
forgetting about me. Sometimes I feel so alone
and like no one cares, and I need to know
that You are there and You love me. Amen.

Be Strong

The LORD Almighty is my strength. He makes my feet
like those of a deer. He makes me walk on the mountains.
HABAKKUK 3:19 (GW)

There will be many times in your life when you feel really weak, like you just can't do whatever it is you're supposed to do. And that's okay. I AM your strength when you are weak, and My power is greater than anything. I want you to need Me so I can help you to be strong.

Sometimes being strong means giving up … giving up your worries and your anger and your fears. You might be facing giants that are making you afraid, you might be looking at a big mountain in front of you that seems impossible to climb. You don't have to do it alone … pray to me and let Me help you do what you think you can't.

Heavenly Father, thank You for loving me
and helping me when I am weak. Give me
the strength to know that I can do anything
with You and nothing is impossible. Amen.

Get Ready

"Get ready; be prepared!"
EZEKIEL 38:7

You don't need to worry about the problems in your life. I will help you—just believe that I will. When life gets hard, I want you to learn to come to Me for help and trust Me by getting ready for My miracles in your life.

When life is difficult, I need you to learn to focus on Me and not be afraid of whatever is going on in your life. Pray to Me, wait on Me, and get ready for My miracles.

Lord, help me not to worry, but to get ready for all the wonderful things You will do in my life. Amen.

I Already Know

"Your heavenly Father already knows."
MATTHEW 6:32

Sometimes you think I'm too busy for you or that I don't care about the small things in your life. But all things are small to Me—I AM God.

If I can keep all the planets moving around the sun, if I keep the whole world together, I can do everything I need to keep your world together.

I know every detail of your life and I know exactly what to do to make sure that everything in your life turns out for good.

Heavenly Father, I will remember that I can pray to
You about anything ... big things and small. Help me
to trust You to do the impossible in my life. Amen.

Just Ask Me

If you need wisdom, ask our generous God,
and He will give it to you.
He will not rebuke you for asking.
JAMES 1:5

When you need anything ... come to Me. Whatever it is ... come to Me and ask. Don't try to figure things out on your own, don't get upset because you don't understand.

I know all, I can do all, just ask Me for help and I will always do what is best for you. Trust Me when you're confused and be calm and sure that I hear you and I will help you.

Lord, I come to You asking for help
because I don't understand my life sometimes.
I'm asking You to help me be at peace
and know that You are with me. Amen.

Seek Me

Search for the Lord and for
His strength; continually seek Him.
1 CHRONICLES 16:11

Many times your troubles get in the way of your relationship with Me. You are so upset and angry that you forget to just come to Me so that I can help you. Your worries can leave you weak and hurting, but spending time with Me will give you peace and strength.

When you play hide-and-seek, it's about finding ... but I'm not hiding—I want you to seek Me and I've promised you'll find Me.

Dear God, I need You to calm my fears
and give me peace so that I am not angry with
all that is wrong in my life. Help me to seek You
always and look to You for strength. Amen.

I Will Hear You

Listen to my cry for help. Pay attention to my prayer.
PSALM 17:1

I hear your cries for help, I know when your heart is breaking. I want you to rest and trust in Me to help you. Don't forget that I do miracles—those things that you think are impossible.

I'm full of surprises. When you pray to Me, trust that I'll take care of you and do whatever needs to be done. I love you more than you will ever know—My help is on the way.

Lord, I need Your help ... I am sad, lonely,
and my heart is breaking. Please love me
and fill me with Your peace. Amen.

Pray All the Time

Pray continually.
1 THESSALONIANS 5:17 (NIV)

When you don't know what to do—pray. When you're not sure what to say—pray. When you feel alone and confused—pray. I want you to pray all the time, talking to Me about everything and asking for My help over and over again.

There's nothing more important in your life than your relationship with Me and there's no one other than Me that can perform the miracles you need and all you must do is pray.

Father, thank You for being there for me.
Thank You for listening to all my prayers.
Please, stay with me forever. Amen.

Be Careful

I don't really understand myself, for I want to do
what is right, but I don't do it. Instead, I do what I hate.
ROMANS 7:15

There will always be chances to do wrong things, and
sometimes wrong things can seem like good things.
That's why I need you to stay close to Me and pray to
Me constantly.

You need help when life is confusing. Just because
you see others doing something, doesn't mean it's the
right thing. I want you to come to Me when you're not
sure what is right or wrong. Don't let anything get in the
way of your relationship with Me.

Heavenly Father, thank You for always
forgiving me when I do wrong things.
I want to always do what makes You smile.
Help me to do right even when it is hard. Amen.

Ask for Forgiveness

"I tell you the truth, unless you turn from
your sins and become like little children,
you will never get into the Kingdom of Heaven."
MATTHEW 18:3

Everyone makes mistakes. But when you make mistakes, I want you to come to Me. I don't want you to feel bad inside when you do wrong things. When you come to Me and talk to Me about what has gone wrong and what you've done, I can forgive you and I can fill you with peace again.

So don't wait when you've done something wrong, don't allow the bad feelings inside to make you feel worse—come to Me and I will forgive all of your mistakes.

Lord God, I mess up and it makes me
feel bad inside. Please help me to remember
to come to You, so that You can forgive me
and I don't have to keep feeling guilty. Amen.

You'll Be Forgiven

He has removed our sins as far from us as the east is from the west. The LORD is like a father to His children, tender and compassionate to those who fear Him.

PSALM 103:12-13

When you feel bad inside from doing wrong things, and making bad choices, you want to run and even hide. Those feelings are called guilt.

Guilt makes you feel bad, but I can help you by taking the guilt away. When you come to Me and tell Me about what is making you feel guilty, I make those bad feelings go away. I use My love to forgive you and help you to know that you can let go of guilt and make better choices.

Lord, thank You for always helping me to let
go of my guilt because You forgive me for
the wrong things I do. I need to know that
You love me even when I mess up. Amen.

Seek My Forgiveness

"I will forgive their wickedness,
and I will never again remember their sins."
JEREMIAH 31:34

I want you to always make good choices, but I know that sometimes it's hard. We all make mistakes. But, I still love you. Nothing can separate you from My love. So don't be afraid to come to Me and tell Me what you've done or why you're feeling bad inside. I already know, but I want you to learn to come to Me and talk to Me, so that I can forgive you and help you.

When you come to Me and you tell Me you are sorry for those wrong things you've done, you can know that I've forgotten it all. I will fill you with My love.

Heavenly Father, I am thankful that even
though I make bad decisions sometimes,
You still love me and help me to let go of my
guilt and start making better choices. Amen.

Run to Me

"Pray that you will not fall into temptation."
LUKE 22:40 (NIV)

You should know that wrong choices begin with wrong thoughts. For you to have right thoughts, you need to always be praying to Me, and always reading the Bible, so you won't believe lies and make wrong choices.

I know it's hard, but you can always come to Me for forgiveness if you make a mistake. What is going on inside you is what comes out. So, I want to fix what is inside of you—I will help you.

Lord, I need Your help so that I do not sin.
Help me to keep my eyes on You and not believe
the lies that take me down wrong paths. Amen.

Be Forgiving

"If you forgive those who sin against you,
your heavenly Father will forgive you."
MATTHEW 6:14

I know it's not easy to forgive others, especially when your feelings get hurt. But you have to remember that you make mistakes and you need forgiveness, too. So, I need your heart to be forgiving, just like My heart is forgiving towards you.

You need to know that forgiving means that the person who has hurt you may not say, "I'm sorry." You need to let your hurt go anyway and know that I will heal your hurting heart.

Lord, help me to forgive others, even when
they really hurt my heart. I want to have peace
and love in my heart all of the time. Amen.

You Are Forgiven

Should we keep on sinning so that God can
show us more and more of His wonderful grace?
ROMANS 6:1

Just because I love you and forgive you, doesn't mean
you should do wrong things. It just means that when you
do make mistakes, you don't have to live with the bad
feelings inside that make you feel guilty. You can come to
Me and I will forgive you.

I want you to stay connected to Me, so that I can help
you make better decisions, but if you do make mistakes,
know that you can come to Me and be forgiven, so that
you can have peace and joy again.

Lord God, help me to do right things. I sometimes
make mistakes and I need to know that You
forgive me so that I can have peace. Amen.

Forgive Others

Jesus said, "Father, forgive them,
for they know not what they do."
LUKE 23:34 (ESV)

Sometimes others will hurt you on purpose. Sometimes they don't really mean to hurt you. Either way, I want you to forgive them by letting go of your anger and wanting to hurt them back.

When you keep holding onto your anger, it makes your life sad and I want you to be happy. So, don't keep being angry—come to Me, pray to Me, and I will help you to forgive.

Dear God, sometimes I feel really hurt and I want
to hurt others back. Help me to let my anger go
and to let You handle the hurt in my life. Amen.

Learn to Forgive

Be kind and compassionate to one another,
forgiving each other, just as in Christ God forgave you.
EPHESIANS 4:32 (NIV)

There will always be times when you get angry because of how others treat you. Sometimes they will say sorry, sometimes they won't. But I need you to forgive anyway.

You have My heart in you and My heart is kind and loving. So, I want you to be kind and loving to others, even when they are not kind and loving to you. I want you to be good to those who are evil because it makes your heart better.

Lord, I get angry when I get hurt and when
others don't say sorry it makes me really upset.
Please fill my heart with Your love so that
I can have peace and live with joy. Amen.

Filled with Peace

"To you who are willing to listen, I say,
love your enemies! Do good to those who hate you.
Bless those who curse you. Pray for those who hurt you."
LUKE 6:27-28

One of the hardest things you'll have to do is forgive someone. Others can be hurtful, even when they don't mean to be. And sometimes they will not even realize they hurt you. But all you need is My love in your heart.

I don't want you to be angry all of the time and hold a grudge. I want you to always have peace. I want you to love those who hate you and pray for those who hurt you and I will bless you.

Heavenly Father, help me to let go of my
anger when others hurt me. Please fill me
with Your peace and help me to love those
who hurt me and are mean to me. Amen.

Trust Me More

We must continue to hold firmly to our declaration
of faith. The one who made the promise is faithful.
HEBREWS 10:23 (GW)

When things don't happen when you think they should
or how you think they should, I know it's hard to trust
that I AM still with you. But if I have made a promise to
you, I will keep it.

There is never a reason for you to worry or be afraid.
I want you to be sure that I AM with you and that I
will answer your prayers. So when it seems like you are
on your own because nothing is happening in your life,
trust Me more and hold on to your faith.

Heavenly Father, help me to hold on to my faith when
I'm doubting and having a hard time in life. Amen.

I Will Never Fail You

Not one word has failed of all the wonderful
promises He gave through His servant Moses.
1 KINGS 8:56

You get worried that I won't help you, that I won't keep
My promises. I know it's because life is hard and sometimes when you pray, you're not sure I'm listening, but I
promise, I AM.

I've made you promises and I do not lie. You should
always know that I will keep My promises even if you do
wrong things, or even if you doubt My power. I will still
keep My promises. So, know that no matter what, I will
never fail you.

Father, sometimes I wonder if You can help me.
My problems seem so big that they are all I see.
Help me remember that You are greater than
any problem, and You'll help me with them.
Because You keep Your promises. Amen.

You Are Safe

The eternal God is your refuge,
and underneath are the everlasting arms.
DEUTERONOMY 33:27 (NIV)

You don't need to see Me or feel My presence to know that I'm with you and holding you. When you are afraid, I want you to pray right away. I want to strengthen you and fill you with hope so you will know that everything is going to be okay.

Even though you don't always see what I AM doing, you can trust that I AM with you … I will help you and I'm holding you.

Dear God, I need to know that You are
holding on to me because I feel so alone
and afraid when life is hard. Amen.

I Hear Your Prayers

With him is only the arm of flesh, but with us is
the LORD our God to help us and to fight our battles.
2 CHRONICLES 32:8 (NIV)

Many days it can seem like you're in a battle. Things in life aren't going right, and no matter what you do, it seems to be wrong.

No matter what, you need to keep praying—that's how battles are won—on your knees, praying. I AM with you throughout it all.

Lord, I need Your help because I feel like
I'm always in a battle and I get tired of
fighting. Help me to rest and know that You
will help me fight these battles. Amen.

I AM Faithful

No temptation has overtaken you except
what is common to mankind. And God is faithful;
He will not let you be tempted beyond what you
can bear. But when you are tempted, He will also
provide a way out so that you can endure it.
1 CORINTHIANS 10:13 (NIV)

You are always going to be tempted to do wrong things.
The devil wants you to believe that lying, cheating, and
doing things to get what you want now, is what is right
for you. But doing wrong things, making decisions without Me, never lead to good things.

So, don't be fooled into thinking that if something
makes you feel good that it is good for you. Sometimes
things will make you feel good, but it's bad for you—it's
against what I've told you to do. Just keep close to Me,
pray to Me when you're confused, and be full of faith.

Heavenly Father, thank You for always helping me to
do right things and forgiving me when I don't. Amen.

Renew Your Heart

I desire to do Your will, my God;
Your law is within my heart.
PSALM 40:8 (NIV)

There will be a lot of things in life that you do not understand, but if you trust Me, I will fill your heart with everything that is in My Word, the Bible, and you won't get frustrated trying to understand. You will just trust Me to be in control and to do what is best.

Your faith in Me puts a new heart in you, filled with My Spirit. I will help you to always want to do what is right and when you make mistakes, you will quickly come to Me to ask for forgiveness.

Heavenly Father, help me to do what is right
and to trust Your Word to lead and guide me. Amen.

My Plans Are for Good

Whatever happens, conduct yourselves in
a manner worthy of the gospel of Christ.
PHILIPPIANS 1:27 (NIV)

Feelings can make things seem like they are out of control, when they're really not. You won't always understand life and that can be confusing. But when you have faith in Me, you can know that I AM in control and there is nothing for you to fear—I AM always in control and My plans for you are always good.

Trusting in Me gives you peace in your heart, even when life is really hard and you're feeling alone, sad, scared, and confused. Come to Me and I will always help, love and protect you no matter what happens.

Lord, my feelings make me feel out of control
and I need You to fill me with Your peace so that
I can have faith no matter what happens. Amen.

Don't Worry

We rely on what Christ Jesus has done for us.
We put no confidence in human effort.
PHILIPPIANS 3:3

I know that it's easy to try and take control of your own life and feel like you can do it on your own, but you can't. Have hope in Me and be confident that I will always take care of you.

When you have troubles in your life, I want you to come to Me first, and know that I will help you. I want you to come to Me and tell Me that you're confused. I want you to trust that I will give you wisdom and help you to know what you should do. Simply trust in Me as your God.

Dear God, help me to remember that You are
God and I'm not. I get confused and afraid and
sometimes I try to take over. Please help me
to trust You to take care of my life. Amen.

Pay Attention

Let those who are wise understand these things. Let those
with discernment listen carefully. The paths of the LORD
are true and right, and righteous people live by walking
in them. But in those paths sinners stumble and fall.

HOSEA 14:9

Things are not always what they seem to be—life can
be confusing and tricky. At times your feelings will make
you feel like things are really bad, and they're not. When
you're confused and frustrated and not sure about what
to do, you need to pay close attention to Me, so that I
can help you.

Learning to listen to Me and hear My voice takes
practice. You must pray and find time where you can sit
silently. Your life doesn't always have to be so noisy. My
will for your life, My desires for you are for you to always
have joy, hope, and peace.

Heavenly Father, help me to always look
to You and pay attention to what You have
taught me through the Bible. Amen.

I Will Guide You

All the believers were one in heart and mind.
ACTS 4:32 (NIV)

I know that life pulls you in a lot of different directions, but I AM always here to help you to make sure you stay on My perfect path for you. Your heart and mind are Mine because you choose to believe in Me.

It's so easy to get sidetracked, but your faith means you're on My path, the believer's path. When you have faith in Me, I give you My heart and My mind ... you have nothing to fear! Don't allow your heart and mind to be divided—you are one with Me, your God—the One who saves you.

Lord, I get confused in life and I lose my way. Help me to come to You when I'm afraid and confused so that You can guide me and give me hope. Amen.

Your Hiding Place

You are my hiding place; You protect me
from trouble. You surround me with songs of victory.
PSALM 32:7

When you are frightened or afraid, you can hide with Me.
I AM your hiding place. I have promised to protect you at
all times and in all ways.

So, I need you to run to Me when you don't know
what to do. I AM with you every step of the way. I will
help you to fight all of your battles. I just want you to be
at peace and trust Me all of the time.

Heavenly Father, thank You for protecting me
and letting me hide with You, so that
I can feel loved and safe. Amen.

Cry Out to Me

I cried out to the LORD in my great
trouble, and He answered me.
JONAH 2:2

I know sometimes you might not think I'm listening, especially when you are in trouble … when nothing is changing.

When your heart is breaking and you're scared and afraid, I will rescue you. When you're in trouble, cry out to Me and I will answer you. It might not happen right away, but I will help you in My perfect way and perfect time.

Lord, sometimes I feel so afraid and I don't
feel like anyone can help me. I am thankful
that I can run to You for help. Amen.

Always Have Hope

As for me, I will always have hope;
I will praise You more and more.
PSALM 71:14 (NIV)

I know that when you're in trouble, it can feel like there is no hope, but there is always hope because I AM God.

When things are hard, you need to continue to pray and have hope. If you're trying to put your hope in anything other than Me, you will be disappointed. So keep reading My Word and praising Me for keeping My promises. There is nothing I can't do.

Heavenly Father, help me to always have
hope even when things seem really bad
and there's nothing I can do about it. Amen.

I Hear Your Cries

I waited patiently for the Lord to help me,
and He turned to me and heard my cry.
PSALM 40:1

Everyone, at some point, needs to be rescued. Things go wrong, life is hard and there are things that you can't do. But I AM on your side and I AM here to help you.

So, when you call to Me, I will help you, but sometimes you must be patient. My plans and miracles don't always happen right away. So keep trusting Me, even when nothing is happening, My help is on the way.

Lord, thank You for rescuing me when
I'm afraid and I don't know what to do.
I AM so thankful for Your love and help. Amen.

I Will Rescue You

Praise to the God of Shadrach, Meshach,
and Abednego! He sent His angel to
rescue His servants who trusted in Him.
DANIEL 3:28

No matter what you are going through, you are never alone. Know that I AM always a prayer away from helping you. I AM always able to rescue you.

Even when you're struggling and feeling like nothing is happening, you should always know that I AM in control—even if things in life are not going well or getting any better.

Heavenly Father, I am so thankful that
You rescue me when life gets out of control.
I pray that You will give me peace to know
that You are always in control. Amen.

Come to Me

> Don't be afraid. Just stand still
> and watch the LORD rescue you today.
>
> EXODUS 14:13

Come to Me when you are afraid. I AM here to give you peace and let you know there is nothing to fear. I AM always in control and I have good things planned for you. So, if things seem confusing and life is too hard and scary, know that I AM always with you …

I will protect you and give you peace. I need you to trust Me and not be afraid.

God, sometimes I don't know what to do and I am
filled with fear about what is going to happen in my
life. I need You to fill me with Your peace so that I can
rest, knowing that You are always in control. Amen.

I'll Protect You

When I am afraid, I put my trust in You.
PSALM 56:3 (NIV)

There will be times when you will feel afraid. It may be because you just don't understand what is going on in your life, or because things aren't going very well and it seems like things are bad and out of control.

If you are feeling afraid, I just want you to pray to Me and focus on Me, instead of your fears. I want you to trust in all of the promises that I've made to you in the Bible. I have promised to always love you and protect you. When you are afraid ... it's time to trust Me and know that everything is okay because I AM God.

Lord, there are so many things that happen in
my life and I often feel afraid. I don't know what
to do and I am scared. Please help me to know
that You are with me and will help me with all
of the things that make me afraid. Amen.

I'll Fight for You

This is what the LORD says: Do not be afraid!
Don't be discouraged by this mighty army,
for the battle is not yours, but God's.
2 CHRONICLES 20:15

Sometimes it might seem like you are in a battle ... you feel like things in your life are too hard and you have to fight all of the time. And then when things are tough, you want a way out and you feel like I'm not helping you.

There is no reason to feel down or afraid, I will help you when you look to Me to fight your battles for you and trust that I will always do what is good for you. It won't always be easy, but I AM bigger than anything ... just trust in Me.

Heavenly Father, help me not to be afraid.
There are so many things in my life that
make me feel scared ... help me to trust in
You to always take care of me. Amen.

Trust in My Love

Such love has no fear, because perfect love
expels all fear. If we are afraid, it is for fear
of punishment, and this shows that we have
not fully experienced His perfect love.

1 JOHN 4:18

I know that you are not perfect, but My love is. I want
you to understand My grace ... it's a gift to you. So no
matter what you do, I still love you. You don't have to do
everything right ... I love you even when you do wrong.

I just want you to come to Me when you know you've
done wrong things ... I don't want you to be afraid. My
love for you is bigger than anything and I promise that
nothing can separate you from My love.

Lord God, thank You that I can be assured that You
love me, that I have nothing to fear and that when
I am afraid, You will fill me with Your peace. Amen.

I'll Make You Strong

The fear of the LORD is the beginning of wisdom,
and knowledge of the Holy One is understanding.
PROVERBS 9:10 (NIV)

Feelings can be hard to deal with. They can get mixed up and make things seem worse than they actually are. Feelings can be really powerful and hard to control, but I want you to know that if you are afraid, it is not a feeling that comes from Me. The Spirit I have given you is a spirit of power, love, and self-control.

So when you are feeling afraid, I want you to use your self-control and remember that your fear is coming from the devil who is trying to trick you into not trusting Me. I want you to keep seeking Me when you are afraid and know that I will make you strong inside and give you peace.

Heavenly Father, my feelings make me so
confused and afraid. Help me to always look to You
and trust You when I don't know what to do. Amen.

A Battle Is Raging

The one who is in you is greater
than the one who is in the world.
1 JOHN 4:4 (NIV)

Most of the time, you think your fights are just with the people and things around you—parents, friends, life that's just going badly. But there is a bigger battle. There is an enemy, the devil. And since you are Mine, he wants to destroy your life or just make you frustrated and angry.

So, first, you need to realize you are in a battle, but it's not always against the things in this world. It's a battle in the spiritual world. To fight these out-of-this-world battles, you must pray and keep praying. Let Me fight your battles for you.

Heavenly Father, I need Your help to fight
my battles because I don't always know what
to do. I will keep praying to You for help so
that I can win the battles in my life. Amen.

Reject Satan's Lies

For every child of God defeats this evil world,
and we achieve this victory through our faith.

1 JOHN 5:4

Don't let all of the things going wrong in your life make you angry and upset. That will only make things worse. I know you might feel angry with Me sometimes for letting these things happen, but you should know that I've promised to take care of you through it all.

Don't believe the devil's lies. He will try to make you believe that everything is your fault or things will never get better. But you know what is truth ... you know what I've promised you ... just trust in what I've promised.

Lord God, please help me to trust in all that
You've told me so that I don't have to be
afraid of the devil and his lies. Amen.

Think About Me

Fix your thoughts on what is true, and honorable
and right, and pure, and lovely, and admirable.
Think about things that are excellent and worthy of praise.
PHILIPPIANS 4:8

You have a lot of thoughts in your head each day. Some good, some bad, and they can make you feel really mixed up. The most important thing is to remember that I AM God.

I AM with you always, so you can't allow your thoughts and your feelings to control you. Remember that I'm in control. Don't let bad thoughts make you do bad things. Think about what you're thinking about and then remember what I've promised you—go to the Bible.

Heavenly Father, help me to think about
everything that is true, pure, right and lovely.
Help me think of You, Lord. Amen.

Let Me Help

Submit yourselves, then, to God.
Resist the devil, and he will flee from you.
JAMES 4:7 (NIV)

There is nothing for you to fear, I AM always with you.
Things may not be going right in your life, but I will help
you through it all. You have an enemy, the devil, but he
can never defeat Me—so you must come to Me for help
and trust Me to help you fight.

You don't need to run or hide—I will help you face
your fears. You must learn to face your fears with your
faith and trust in My power to save you.

Dear God, help me not to fear.
Things in my life are hard and I am afraid of
being alone. Help me to know that You are
with me always and You will protect me. Amen.

Rely on My Power

This is not a wrestling match against a human
opponent. We are wrestling with rulers, authorities,
the powers who govern this world of darkness,
and spiritual forces that control evil in the heavenly world.

EPHESIANS 6:12 (GW)

I know that it's easy to believe that you are wrestling, fighting, with parents or friends, and even enemies; but there is only one enemy that you need to focus on— it's the devil that wants to trick you—he's the one you're wrestling with.

When you must fight against powers not in your world, you must fight them with My Word, Truth. Know that when you feel frustrated. You need to pray to Me so that you have all of My power to help you.

Lord God, thank You for helping me fight my battles
and giving me strength to have faith that You will
keep me safe against all that is evil. Amen.

Listen Carefully

You will hear a voice behind you saying, "This is the way.
Follow it, whether it turns to the right or to the left."
ISAIAH 30:21 (GW)

I know that it's hard when you can't hear My voice "out loud", speaking, like you'd like to hear Me, but that doesn't mean I'm not speaking. Sometimes I speak to your spirit and your heart, sometimes I speak to you through other people in your life.

You should always be looking for Me in your life, always be listening, and know that I AM with you always. I will speak to you about big things and small things. I care about everything in your life ... be still and listen for My voice.

Lord God, help me to listen for Your voice,
to be still and know that You will speak
to me when I pray to You. Amen.

Where to Go

"I will instruct you and teach you in the way
you should go; I will counsel you [who are
willing to learn] with My eye upon you."
PSALM 32:8 (AMP)

There are many different ways you can live your life. There are many choices you will have to make. The wrong way can sometimes seem like the right way because wrong things sometimes seem fun.

But that's why I've given you My Spirit inside you, so that you will not be lied to, so that you will hear My voice to help you know which way to go; because My way is the only way that will give you peace and happiness.

Heavenly Father, help me to follow the path
that You want for me. When I'm confused,
please speak to me so that I do not go down
wrong roads which can harm me. Amen.

Watch for Surprises

Jesus said, "Blessed rather are those
who hear the word of God and keep it!"
LUKE 11:28 (ESV)

I want you to have an exciting life that is full of My surprises. Life won't always be easy, and there will be troubles, but I work miracles and I can turn bad things into good things.

When you're not sure about life and things are confusing and hard, know that you don't have to have everything figured out … you know Me and I know everything. Just be at peace, pray to Me and watch for My surprises.

Lord, help me to hear Your voice, to look for miracles,
and expect You to show up when I need You. Amen.

Listen for the Truth

"The thief comes only in order to steal and kill
and destroy. I came that they may have and enjoy life,
and have it in abundance [to the full, till it overflows]."
JOHN 10:10 (AMP)

Sometimes it will be really hard to tell the difference between the truth and a lie. It's easy to live your life based on how you feel. Feelings and emotions are very strong, so you must always ask what the Bible says about your situations in life.

I've given you the Bible as your instruction book for life. The Bible gives you My promises, so that you can be sure of what is the truth and what is a lie. So, when you're confused, come to Me, read My Word, the Bible, and you will know the truth.

Dear God, it's hard sometimes to know what
is the truth and what is a lie, please help
me to know the difference with the help of
Your Spirit, so that I do not sin. Amen.

Walk This Way

Let those who are wise understand these things.
Let those with discernment listen carefully.
The paths of the LORD are true and right,
and righteous people live by walking in them.
But in those paths sinners stumble and fall.

HOSEA 14:9

I know that faith is hard. It's easier to believe in what you can see instead of what you can't. Faith means that you trust in Me without seeing Me, it means you believe in the Bible and that it is My voice speaking to you, telling you which way to go, what to do, or what to say.

You won't always understand things in your life, which is why you need My help. So pray to me and keep praying. Call on Me and I will answer you.

Lord, faith is really hard sometimes.
I want to believe, but sometimes I doubt.
Help me to read Your Word and listen to what
it says so that I will do what is right. Amen.

My Grace Is Enough

"My grace is all you need.
My power works best in weakness."
2 CORINTHIANS 12:9

I know that when you do wrong things, you don't think you deserve to be loved and forgiven, but I always forgive when you come to Me. And when you come to Me, I can give you My grace—grace is My love and forgiveness even if you don't deserve it.

My grace is all you need. So don't think that just because you make a mistake that you are all alone—you are never alone ... I AM always with you.

Dear God, thank You for Your love that
forgives me and sets me free from all of
my wrong choices. Help me to have
more faith and rely on Your grace. Amen.

Nothing Is Impossible

"I am the Lord God of all humanity.
Nothing is too hard for Me."
JEREMIAH 32:27 (GW)

Sometimes the troubles in your life might seem too big, but nothing is too big for Me—I can do anything—nothing is too hard for Me.

I want you to learn to come to Me when life is hard and you feel all alone. Always remember that I AM with you. Always know that I love you and will help you in whatever ways you need Me.

Lord, I am so thankful that You are my God and that there is nothing You can't do ... I can always hope for the impossible because of Your love for me. Amen.

I'll Strengthen You

It is God who arms me with strength
and keeps my way secure.
PSALM 18:32 (NIV)

When you feel alone, I know that you feel weak. When you think there is no one to help you, it's easy to feel like nothing is going to get better and things will only get worse. But I AM with you to give you hope.

I know all about your dreams, all that you wish for. I want you to have good things in life, but sometimes that means trusting Me in the hard times too. I will make you stronger as you learn to come to Me and trust Me.

Heavenly Father, thank You for giving me strength
when I am weak and feeling all alone. Help me to be
sure of the hope that You've promised to me. Amen.

Full of Power

For the word of God is living and active and full of power.
HEBREWS 4:12 (AMP)

I think sometimes you forget that My power lives within you. Through your faith, when you believe in Me, I AM always with you, living in you, to help you in every way.

But you must trust in My promises, which is My Word, the Bible. My Word is alive, it has power and accomplishes all that I have promised it will.

So, I want you to always trust in Me so that My power will always be inside of you.

Lord God, fill me with hope in the
promises of Your Word and help me
to always trust You as my God. Amen.

Stand Firm

Stand firm and hold fast to the
teachings we passed on to you.
2 THESSALONIANS 2:15 (NIV)

At times, life will be very hard. It will be really hard to tell what is truth and what is a lie, which is why I want you to always be seeking Me and making sure you are getting advice from Me.

I want you to always get your strength from Me—always pray to Me, read the Bible and listen for Me to speak to you in your heart. When life is hard and confusing, know that I AM always with you … I will always help you.

Heavenly Father, when life is hard,
help me to hold on to You. I want to know
You better and have stronger faith. Amen.

My Love Is Perfect

God showed His great love for us by sending
Christ to die for us while we were still sinners.
ROMANS 5:8

You cannot imagine how much I love you. And I know sometimes, because life is so hard, you wonder if I even love you at all. My love for you never fails and it never ends. Even when you make mistakes, I still love you.

You can always come to Me and I will forgive you. Jesus died on the cross to save you, so that your sins can be forgiven and you don't have to feel guilty. That's what My love does for you and there is no greater love.

Heavenly Father, thank You for loving me no matter what mistakes I make. I need to know that I can always come to You for help. Amen.

Saved by Grace

Because of His great love for us, God who is rich in mercy,
made us alive with Christ even when we were dead in
transgressions—it is by grace you have been saved.
EPHESIANS 2:4-5 (NIV)

I know that you feel like you're always having to work
so hard to do right things and you just feel like life is too
difficult and you just can't do it. And often times, because of your mistakes, you feel like you don't deserve
to be loved.

But that's what grace is for. Grace means I give you
My love and forgiveness, even if you don't think you deserve it. So come to Me when you need love ... I will
always love you—no matter what.

Lord God, thank You for Your grace that
saves me. Thank You that I can have peace
that You love me no matter what. Amen.

Flooded with Light

I pray that your hearts will be flooded with light
so that you can understand the confident hope
He has given to those He called—His holy people
who are His rich and glorious inheritance.
EPHESIANS 1:18

When you're weak, I can make you strong. I AM with you always to help you step-by-step with whatever you need help with in life. You can always come to Me when you are feeling down or afraid and when life's problems make things seem dark and gloomy.

My love can flood the darkness with light. I AM all you need, you just need to come to Me, praying, and expecting Me to help you.

Dear God, sometimes I feel really weak
and I lose hope. Please help me to remember
that I don't have a reason to be sad
because You will fix everything. Amen.

Holding You Close

Even if my father and mother
abandon me, the Lᴏʀᴅ will hold me close.
PSALM 27:10

Sometimes you will feel unloved. You may not feel loved by family or even friends—but you are always loved by Me. Even when you make mistakes, even when you've really done wrong things, you can always come to Me and I will love you.

So even though it might seem like others have abandoned you, and it feels like no one cares, you can be sure that I never stop loving you and I AM always holding you close.

Lord God, sometimes I feel unloved and I need
to know that You still love me. I don't like it when
I do wrong things, but I make mistakes and I
am thankful that I can come to You. Amen.

Give Your Heart

Seek the LORD your God with all your heart and soul.
1 CHRONICLES 22:19

I love you more than you will ever know. You were created to know Me, to walk with Me through this life, and to look forward to spending eternity with Me.

You will never fully understand how much I love you and all of the amazing plans I have for your life. I AM all you need to experience the peace and joy you're supposed to have in life. But I need you to completely trust Me. Keep seeking Me with all of your heart and soul.

Heavenly Father, help me to understand how
much You love me, so that I can have peace
and joy even when life is hard. Amen.

Don't Give Up

Don't lose your confidence. It will bring you
a great reward. You need endurance so that
after you have done what God wants you to do,
you can receive what He has promised.
HEBREWS 10:35-36 (GW)

I want you to remember to never give up. Don't lose hope just because things aren't going the way you want them to. I know that it's hard to keep hoping when bad things keep happening. But if you'll stay focused on Me, I will remind you of all the reasons to keep believing—the biggest reason is that I AM God and I can do anything.

Just because you have trouble in your life, does not mean that I've left your side. Just keep waiting for Me and expecting Me to show up—just don't give up.

Lord, help me not to lose hope, but to know that
You can do anything and I should not give up. Amen.

Keep Hoping

As for me, I look to the LORD for help. I wait confidently
for God to save me, and my God will certainly hear me.
MICAH 7:7

You might feel helpless, like there is nothing you can do
to fix the problems in your life, but that doesn't mean
you should stop believing because it seems like there is
no hope.

The things I allow in your life, the plans I have for
you won't always make sense to you. Don't try to figure
everything out. I want you to learn to trust Me no matter
what—when things are good and when things are bad.
Just keep hoping in Me.

Heavenly Father, sometimes I feel helpless and alone.
I need to know that everything is going to
be okay and that You are with me always. Amen.

Nothing Can Separate Us

Nothing can ever separate us from God's love.
ROMANS 8:38

I know that sometimes life can get really scary. There will be times when you feel that all hope is gone and you are just a victim to all of the bad things in the world. But you are Mine and I will always protect you and take care of you.

There is absolutely nothing that can touch you without My permission. If I allow tough things in your life, I have promised that they are for reasons that I will use for good, in the end. So, trust Me and do not fear. I AM with you always.

Heavenly Father, help me not to fear
anything in my life, but to constantly look
to You for my peace and strength. Amen.

Peace of Mind and Heart

"I am leaving you with a gift—peace of mind
and heart. And the peace I give is a gift the world
cannot give. So don't be troubled or afraid."
JOHN 14:27

When you are afraid, come to Me right away. Do not waste time and energy worrying and being afraid. I AM in control of all things.

When you are losing hope, when you're not sure if everything is going to be okay, it's My Spirit that will fill you with unimaginable peace. You might still be going through tough times, but I will be with you and I will comfort you and give you strength to continue to believe.

Lord God, thank You for the gift of
Your peace in the middle of all my troubles.
I am grateful for all of Your gifts. Amen.

Be Worry-Free

Worry weighs a person down.
PROVERBS 12:25

Life is hard enough without having to worry too. I know that you think that there is nothing you can do when you have trouble in your life, but you can do something ... the best thing ... pray.

Pray to Me about everything that is bothering you ... everything that is making you afraid and worried. I can give you peace, I can speak to your heart and calm you. I can give you My grace so that you can rest knowing that I will take care of you and all of your troubles. Don't become more afraid by worrying, focus on My promises to you ... I will work all things together for good.

Dear God, help me not to worry so much,
but to focus on Your promises and
be at peace knowing that You have
everything under control. Amen.

Don't Worry, Be Happy

"Can all your worries add a single moment to your life?"
MATTHEW 6:27

I know that when your life is hard, it is easy to worry. But try not to focus on your problems. I need you to focus on Me and all of the promises I've made you.

You will find that there will always be problems in life that will make you want to worry. Your worries don't mean anything when you have My promises. I don't want you wasting your time worrying. Let Me handle all of your problems—trust Me to do miracles.

Lord God, help me not to worry, but to trust that
You have everything under control and You only
have good things planned for my life. Amen.

God's Goodness

I believe that I will see the goodness
of the LORD in this world of the living.
PSALM 27:13 (GW)

I want to bless you more than anything you can hope
for or imagine. You can believe in My goodness. I have
promised you that I will work all things together for good.

I know it's not always easy to believe in Me and all
that I've promised you—especially when things seem to
get worse and not better. I AM working in your life, you
will find that sometimes things might look bad, but I AM
using them for good. Believe it, and you will see.

Heavenly Father, thank You for Your goodness,
for Your love and kindness and the promises
You've made to me to give me hope. Amen.

Unshakable Faith

Declare me innocent, O LORD, for I have acted
with integrity; I have trusted in the LORD without wavering.
PSALM 26:1

Everything that happens in your life, the big things and the small things, will require My help. Constantly pray to Me, so that your faith will be unshakable.

You won't always be able to control what is going on in your life, but you can completely trust Me to always be in control ... to love you, to help you, to protect you, to give you hope. I want you to always have faith and joy. Know that I AM with you always.

Lord God, help me to trust that You are
God all the time, not just sometimes.
Fill me with faith so that I will not fear. Amen.

Just Remember ...

But then I recall all You have done, O Lord;
I remember Your wonderful deeds of long ago.
They are constantly in my thoughts. I cannot
stop thinking about Your mighty works.

PSALM 77:11-12

It won't always be easy to keep believing and having hope when things don't seem to be getting better. So, you will need to be constantly seeking Me and paying attention to My Word, the Bible.

You cannot decide to believe only when things are going your way, you must always believe. And if you have a hard time, just remember the ways I have helped you in the past and how I've answered your prayers before— know that I will continue to bless you.

Dear God, I remember all of the little prayers You've
answered and all of the big ones. Help me to have
faith even when it's hard to believe sometimes. Amen.

Live By Faith

"My righteous ones will live by faith. But I will
take no pleasure in anyone who turns away."
HEBREWS 10:38

You need to have faith for My power to work in your life.
Truly believe in the promises I've made to you. That's
where My power is.

Don't rely on your feelings and emotions to decide
whether or not you believe because feelings and emotions can trick you. That is why you should always pray
to Me right away, so that I can lead and guide you with
My Spirit. There's no reason to be worried or afraid—all
you need is faith.

Heavenly Father, thank You for the strength
You give me to keep believing even when I'm
feeling doubtful. Help me not to worry. Amen.

God Is in Control

"For as the heavens are higher than
the earth, so are My ways higher than your
ways and My thoughts than your thoughts."
ISAIAH 55:9 (ESV)

I know that when life is hard, you can get very confused.
You don't understand why I don't do certain things or do
them at a certain time and way. But you can't understand
because you aren't able to see the big picture like I can.
So, you must trust Me.

Don't let yourself give in to bad thoughts, getting frustrated and angry trying to control things that you can't
control. Only I can control everything. I need you to trust
in My ways and know that I will always do what is best
for you. I'm full of surprises—just keep believing in Me.

Lord God, help me to be at peace
knowing that You have everything under
control and You know what is best. Amen.

I AM Here to Help

"In that way, you will be acting as true children
of your Father in heaven. For He gives His
sunlight to both the evil and the good, and He
sends rain on the just and the unjust alike."

MATTHEW 5:45

I don't want you to stop believing in Me just because life gets hard and bad things happen. I AM with you during the good things and the bad. I know that when you're afraid or sad and things aren't getting better, you don't know if you really believe in Me. But you must keep believing.

This is how your faith grows. I need you to believe most when things get really hard. You can't just believe when life is easy. Come to Me always—I'm waiting for you.

Heavenly Father, thank You for the good
things You give and thank You for helping
me with the hard things in life. Amen.

I Will Bless You

"Test Me in this way," says the Lord of Armies.
"See if I won't open the windows of heaven
for you and flood you with blessings."
MALACHI 3:10 (GW)

Life is full of things that don't go the way you want them to. Sometimes friends can hurt your feelings or decide not to be your friend anymore. But don't get discouraged.

Don't let yourself think bad thoughts. I want you to know I AM with you and you need to trust Me to bless you, to give you good things—to bring good things from bad. You need to keep believing that I AM in control and I will always help you and do what is best for you.

Heavenly Father, thank You for all of the ways
that You bless me. Help me to trust in You
and believe in You for bigger things. Amen.

Peace from God

They were all terrified when they saw Him.
But Jesus spoke to them at once. "Don't be
afraid," He said. "Take courage! I am here!"
MARK 6:50

There are so many things in life that can go wrong. Sometimes it will seem like nothing is going right. It's when things are really hard that you need My peace and rest.

I need you to pray when you're afraid, trust Me when you don't know what to do, and believe in Me even when you're not sure you should. When you pray, I listen, and I answer you. There is nothing to be afraid of, I AM with you, you can be at peace and rest.

Lord God, all I need is You. Help me to be
at peace and have rest, knowing that You are
with me in the good times and the bad. Amen.

Get to Know Me

They strengthened the disciples in these
cities and encouraged the disciples to remain
faithful. Paul and Barnabas told them, "We
must suffer a lot to enter God's kingdom."
ACTS 14:22 (GW)

I know you have lots of questions. You want to know "why" things happen and "why" things are the way they are. I know it's hard to believe in Me when you just don't understand. But I have given you faith, so that you can be strong and believe, even when you're confused about life.

Sometimes you will understand what I AM doing, but sometimes you will not. I want you to learn to pray to Me, I want you to know Me better so that your faith will grow stronger.

Lord God, please strengthen me and help me
to have faith even when I don't always understand.
Thank You for always loving me
and helping me. Amen.

Be Patient

O Lord, how long will You forget me?
PSALM 13:1

When you pray, I know that sometimes it can seem like I don't hear you or My answers are taking too long. I know that you think you need things "right now", but sometimes waiting is better.

There's no reason for you to be sad or discouraged when My miracles don't happen right away—I want you to trust Me, even when it seems like nothing is going to happen. That's what faith is and true faith keeps believing no matter how long it takes.

Lord, I feel like You've forgotten me and it doesn't
seem like You are going to answer my prayers.
Please give me patience, Father. Amen.

Trust Jesus

Commit everything you do to the LORD.
Trust Him, and He will help you.
PSALM 37:5

While you're waiting on your prayers to be answered, I want you to have faith, while you're waiting. I know it's hard to believe that your prayers will be answered, when you can't see things changing.

But while you're waiting, I want you to be thankful, to be looking for ways to help others and be kind. Waiting in faith doesn't mean doing nothing.

Heavenly Father, while I wait on Your
answers to my prayers, help me to do the
things You want me to as I wait. Amen.

Perfect Timing

"At the right time, I, the Lord, will make it happen."
ISAIAH 60:22

When you have to wait on Me, you learn how much faith you do or don't have. Sometimes I use your "waiting" times to teach you to trust Me more, and not to give up.

So don't always think that just because you don't see Me answering your prayers right away that the miracles you're praying for aren't going to happen. Faith in Me keeps trusting, even if things get worse before they get better. Trust that My miracles will come at just the right time. My timing is perfect.

Lord God, help me to have faith to trust
that You will answer my prayers when
You think it is the best time. Amen.

Stay Thankful

Because of our faith, Christ has brought us into this place
of undeserved privilege where we now stand, and we
confidently and joyfully look forward to sharing God's glory.
ROMANS 5:2

When you're waiting, I want you to enjoy each and every day. I don't want you waiting and being sad and discouraged. I want you to live each day with joy and happiness, knowing that I will answer your prayers.

I've given you each day to be happy and know that even when things are really hard, everything is going to be okay. Keep looking up to Me, keep praying, and keep being thankful, each and every day.

Heavenly Father, help me to have joy,
even as I wait on You to answer my prayers.
Fill me with hope and gratitude. Amen.

You Need Me

As the deer pants for streams of water,
so my soul pants for You, my God.
PSALM 42:1 (NIV)

You may not realize it, but waiting on Me will help you to see how much you need Me. When you need Me, it draws you closer to Me and makes our relationship stronger.

So when you have to wait, it may seem hard and like you are waiting for nothing, but if you will use those times of waiting to seek Me more, you will not waste time waiting. Waiting for Me is needing Me and you'll learn that you can always count on My miracles.

Lord, I truly need You and I feel like hope
is gone. Please have mercy on my heart
and fill my soul with Your Spirit. Amen.

Listen and Search

They listened eagerly ... They searched the Scriptures day
after day to see if Paul and Silas were teaching the truth.

ACTS 17:11

Having a relationship with Me is the most important thing
in your life. I want you to pray to Me about everything
and listen for My answers. Sometimes the answers will be
easy, at other times it will be hard to know what to do.

I want you to keep searching for My answers. Don't
give up when things are hard. I can do really amazing
miracles when things are really bad. So keep looking to
Me, I will always help you.

Heavenly Father, help me to listen for Your voice in
my heart. Strengthen me when things are hard and
help me to keep believing no matter what. Amen.

Pray for Help

"Be strong and very courageous. Be careful
to obey all the law My servant Moses gave you;
do not turn from it to the right or to the left,
that you may be successful wherever you go."

JOSHUA 1:7 (NIV)

To obey Me means to listen to what I tell you to do in the Bible. It's not always easy to do all that I ask you to do. When you're angry or upset, it's even harder to do the right thing, so you need to always pray to Me as soon as you're confused and not feeling right inside.

It is very important for you to be strong, brave, and careful to obey Me. When you feel like things aren't going right, remember I AM with you always to help you and give you hope.

Lord God, I come to You praying for help. At times,
I just don't know what to do and I need to know that
You are with me and that I don't need to worry. Amen.

Look to Me

He who has compassion on them will guide
them and lead them beside springs of water.
ISAIAH 49:10 (NIV)

When you have to decide between right and wrong, I need you to pray to Me and sit quietly with Me. I love you and I always want what is best for you, but you must make your relationship and time with Me the first priority in your life.

Look to Me, listen to Me, and trust Me, even when life is confusing and doesn't make sense. I will always work all things together for good.

Heavenly Father, thank You for Your compassion,
the love You give me and how You always
take care of me. Help me to always put my
relationship with You first in my life. Amen

Come Alive in Me

Teach me Your ways, O LORD, that I may
live according to Your truth! Grant me purity
of heart, so that I may honor You.
PSALM 86:11

When you decide to believe in Me, I put My Spirit in you. I AM alive in you. It's through the Bible that you learn about Me and what is right and wrong. It's My Spirit in you that will remind you of all that I've taught you in the Bible.

When you pray to Me, when you don't know what to do, I have promised to strengthen you, make you wise, and always help you in all the ways you need Me to.

Lord, teach Me how to live the life You
want me to and help me to always
remember that You are alive in me. Amen.

Truth vs. Lies

All Your words are true; all Your righteous laws are eternal.
PSALM 119:160 (NIV)

Sometimes it's really hard to tell what is the truth and what is a lie. Things and people in the world can be very tricky. That's why I've given you the Bible and My Spirit within you so that I can help you.

If you've done something wrong … come to Me. If you're confused by what is true and what is a lie … come to Me. I will always help you to see the truth and I will always lead and guide you to make the right decisions.

Heavenly Father, thank You for the Bible that helps me to know what is the truth and what is a lie. Help me to always seek You when I don't know what to do. Amen.

Get Up!

And we know that God causes everything to work
together for the good of those who love God and
are called according to His purpose for them.
ROMANS 8:28

Sometimes, when things aren't going well for you, you're tempted to get down and discouraged and nothing can make you happy. But sometimes, you just have to decide to "get up", to do things that you love doing, so that you aren't so sad.

Life is not always going to be easy and things won't always go the way you want them to, but I've promised to work all things together for good. Everything will be okay.

Lord God, please help me when I'm
discouraged and unhappy. Fill me with
peace and joy when life is hard. Amen.

I'll Make a Way

Some men came carrying a paralyzed man on a
mat and tried to take him into the house to lay him
before Jesus. When they could not find a way to do
this because of the crowd, they went up on the roof
and lowered him on his mat through the tiles into
the middle of the crowd, right in front of Jesus.

LUKE 5:18-19 (NIV)

It may seem like there is no way to fix a situation or get through it. But when you're stuck, know that I will always make a way. All you must do is trust Me and not give up. Don't stop praying and hoping.

My ways may not always be easy, and you may not always be able to escape problems, but I will always be with you and make a way through it all. And along the way I will give you joy, peace, and happiness.

Heavenly Father, sometimes it seems to me
that my problems are even impossible for You.
Help me to trust in Your Word that
nothing is impossible for You. Amen.

Don't Look Back

Jesus told him, "Anyone who puts a hand to the plow
and then looks back is not fit for the Kingdom of God."
LUKE 9:62

I know that sometimes you get focused on the past, what
you've done right and all that's gone wrong. I want you
with Me—right now—focusing on My love for you and not
being discouraged by the problems in your life.

I will always help you, so do not fear. Just trust Me, do
all that I ask you to do ... and don't look back ... always
be looking forward in faith.

Lord, help me to keep my eyes on You and to always
focus on the good things in my life, and not on all of
my problems that will one day disappear. Amen.

Raise You Up

The LORD Himself goes before you and will be with you;
He will never leave you nor forsake you.
Do not be afraid; do not be discouraged.
DEUTERONOMY 31:8 (NIV)

Don't allow yourself to be discouraged and full of fear—
make sure you're focusing on the good things in your life.
Think about what is true, what is right, what is good.

Many times your feelings get in the way of your faith
in Me and you get sad and can't seem to be happy. When
you're down and feeling all alone, remember to pray and
to trust Me to fill you with My love. I will lift you out of
the pit.

Dear God, I feel like I'm in a pit that I can't get out of.
Life is too hard and I need hope.
Please help me to know that You love me. Amen.

Look Straight Ahead

Look straight ahead, and fix
your eyes on what lies before you.
PROVERBS 4:25

There will be a lot of disappointments in your life. Sometimes life is hard because of things you do, sometimes it's just because things go wrong. But whatever is causing you to be down, if it's something you've done, your wrongs can be made right, and I will use all the bad things in your life for good.

I just want you to keep your eyes on Me and keep believing. When life is too hard for you, it's never too hard for Me—just trust Me and look straight ahead to all of the good things I have in store for you.

Lord God, help me to look forward to the
hope that You give me. It's so easy for me to
look at how hard life is, instead of all of the
blessings You have promised to me. Amen.

Choose Peace

Make every effort to live in peace ... and to be
holy; without holiness no one will see the Lord.
HEBREWS 12:14 (NIV)

There will be so many things in life that make you feel
afraid, worried, or disappointed. All of these things try to
steal your peace and make you feel like things are bad
and will never get better.

But if you are hoping in Me, you can have My peace
all of the time. My peace doesn't care what is going on in
life, My peace is the same no matter what ... and you can
have My peace if you keep trusting Me, even when you're
not sure you can.

Lord God, thank You for Your peace that helps
me to be calm even when life is not. Amen.

You'll Find Rest

The LORD gives strength to His people;
the LORD blesses His people with peace.
PSALM 29:11 (NIV)

When you're frustrated and tired of life, when you are worried and afraid, it is trusting in Me that will give you the peace you need to rest. I want you to learn to rely on Me and rest, even when there are lots of troubles in life.

Every time something goes wrong in life, you should use that time to remind yourself to come to Me, to trust in Me, so that I can help you more. If you will come to Me, I will always give you all the grace, peace, and strength you need.

Heavenly Father, I get frustrated and tired and
want to give up. Please help me to rely on
You and Your strength, so that I can be calm
and peaceful when life is hard. Amen.

My Perfect Peace

"You will keep in perfect and constant peace
the one whose mind is steadfast [that is, committed
and focused on You—in both inclination and
character], Because he trusts and takes refuge in
You [with hope and confident expectation]."
ISAIAH 26:3 (AMP)

Things in your life might change, but I do not change. I AM the same yesterday, today, and forever. I know that sometimes you get frustrated with your life and you feel like all you do is cry because of your sadness, but know that I AM with you through it all, I catch every tear.

Even when life is hard, even when things don't get better, you need to trust Me and be filled with hope and peace. Know that even though you might feel alone, you are not. I AM always with you and working on all that is important in your life.

Lord, please give me Your peace, I feel restless
and I am having a hard time calming down
because of how crazy life feels. Amen.

Find Peace

I pray that God, the source of hope, will fill you
completely with joy and peace because you trust
in Him. Then you will overflow with confident
hope through the power of the Holy Spirit.
ROMANS 15:13

Life can get difficult in a hurry and it's hard to make good
decisions when your feelings are messed up with anger,
sadness or fear.

So, know that if you're having a hard time believing,
I will strengthen you and give you peace to keep having
faith and to believe in Me to help you with everything in
your life. I just need you to keep believing and I will fill
you with hope and joy and give you peace in believing.

Heavenly Father, I need Your peace
because my feelings keep me from thinking
straight and hearing Your voice. Strengthen
me and help me to believe. Amen.

Seek Me

Seek peace and pursue it.
PSALM 34:14 (AMP)

You need to have My peace so that you can have peace with others. And in order to have My peace, you have to seek it, because it will be hard to find peace when things in life aren't going right and when things seem unfair.

But you should always know that you can have My peace if you will pray to Me. I will always help you with whatever you need Me to and I will always give you strength and peace when you are tired and weak. All you need to do is seek Me.

Lord, help me to seek Your peace and to be calm
even when life is hard and unfair. Help me to
focus on You and not on my problems. Amen.

Talk to Me

Pray in the Spirit at all times and on
every occasion. Stay alert and be persistent
in your prayers for all believers everywhere.
EPHESIANS 6:18

I want you to pray all of the time. Not just when you need something. Praying brings you closer to Me and it keeps you from worrying so much.

Anywhere you are, at any time, you can pray. So whatever is bothering you, whatever is making you sad, I want you to talk to Me about it so you don't stay sad. I want you to let Me handle everything that makes you worry, so that you can have fun and enjoy your life.

Heavenly Father, help me to pray all of the time and
come to You when I am confused and afraid. Amen.

Let Me Handle It

Turn your burdens over to the Lord, and He will take care
of you. He will never let the righteous person stumble.
PSALM 55:22 (GW)

Sometimes you can get stuck thinking about all of the
things that are wrong. You keep feeling upset and can't
seem to feel happy or have fun.

I want you to learn to give up all of those bad things
and let Me handle them. I want you to always know that
you can trust Me with whatever is bothering you. I will
help you with everything that is making you worried. Let
Me help you.

Lord, help me to give You all of my worries.
I want to let go of my problems so that
I can enjoy the life You've given me. Amen.

What If?

Get ready; be prepared.
EZEKIEL 38:7 (NIV)

There's no reason for you to be worried or afraid when you have troubles in your life. Everything is going to be okay because I'm in control and I can do anything.

Don't let yourself keep thinking "what if". "What ifs" will only keep your mind from believing in Me.

When you have bad, worried thoughts, stop and pray to Me so that I can give your mind peace. Then you can get ready for all of the good things I have planned.

Dear God, help me to stay focused on You and look forward to the great plans You have for my life. Help me to not think about "what ifs". Amen.

Take a Deep Breath

Praise be to the Lord, to God our Savior,
who daily bears our burdens.
PSALM 68:19 (NIV)

Your burdens, those things that you worry about, those problems that keep you from going to sleep at night, are things I should be dealing with.

So, I want you to take a deep breath and give me all of the things that are bothering you. I want you to enjoy your life and have hope because of the promises I've made you.

Lord, sometimes I can't sleep at night because
I am so worried about the problems in my life.
Help me to remember that You can handle
anything and everything. Amen.

I'll Give You Hope

"Then you will know that I am the LORD your God
who has freed you from your oppression."

EXODUS 6:7

I don't want you to lose hope because of all of your worries. Your mind will play tricks on you and make you feel like things are worse than they are.

When you are feeling afraid of the future and what is going to happen, I want you to look up and pray to Me ... knowing that I will help you. I can bring you out of your sadness and fill you with joy and peace. No matter what is happening in your life, just come to Me.

Heavenly Father, I feel like there is no hope
when life gets really hard. My mind keeps
telling me that nothing is going to get better.
Please fill my heart with hope. Amen.

Change Your Thoughts

For as he thinks in his heart, so is he.
PROVERBS 23:7 (AMP)

I know that when life isn't going just right, it's easy to think about the bad things instead of all of the good things in your life. You have to constantly think about what you're thinking about—because your mind can get filled with bad things really fast.

So when your mind wanders, when you're confused and thinking negative thoughts, remember to pray and ask for My help to get your mind thinking things that are good.

Lord, sometimes my mind gets stuck thinking
bad thoughts, help me to focus on You and
think things that are good. Amen.

Give Thanks

I am not saying this because I am in need,
for I have learned to be content whatever the
circumstances. I know what it is to be in need,
and I know what it is to have plenty.
PHILIPPIANS 4:11-12 (NIV)

I know that there are lots of things you want or need, and I will always take care of you, but you have to learn to be happy with what you have before I give you more.

So when things are good, you can be really glad. When things are bad, pray and know that I will make sure that you have all you need.

Heavenly Father, I am so thankful for all that
You give me in life. Help me to always praise
You whether I have a little or a lot. Amen.

I Will Bless You

The fear of the Lord leads to life, and whoever has
it rests satisfied; he will not be visited by harm.
PROVERBS 19:23 (ESV)

I know it's hard not to want more and more in life, but I
need you to learn to be happy with what you have. Sometimes I bless you with things. Sometimes I will just bless
you with peace and joy.

But there is no reason for you to worry, I will always
take care of you. I will always make sure that you have
enough faith to keep believing that I have everything
under control and everything is going to be okay.

Lord God, I worry a lot because things in life
go wrong and I'm scared that things are not
going to turn out right. Please help me to simply
trust You and Your love for me. Amen.

Focus On Me

Those who seek the LORD lack no good thing.
PSALM 34:10 (ESV)

I know you worry about a lot of things in life, but I want you to let Me worry about all of the things in your life. I just want you to stay focused on Me, and enjoy your life.

You might not know all of My plans for your life, but you can be sure that they are for your good. So, enjoy your life, be happy, and know that there is nothing good that I will not give to you.

Heavenly Father, help me not to worry
so much and to just stay focused on You.
Help me to enjoy my life and be happy. Amen.

Be Happy

A heart at peace gives life to the body,
but envy rots the bones.
PROVERBS 14:30 (NIV)

I know it's hard not to want things, but I want you to learn to be happy with what you've been given because being thankful will give you a happy heart.

When you always want what others have and what you don't have, it makes your heart feel bad and takes away your joy. I want you to know that I will give you special things that others don't have. I will give you what you need and others what they need. So be thankful and you'll be happy.

Lord, help me to be happy with what I have
and to have a thankful heart. Amen.

I Can Do All Things

Put your trust in the LORD.
PSALM 4:5 (ESV)

Life is hard, but you are not alone. I know it's easy to feel alone, but you are never alone, I have promised to be with you always. It might seem like there is no hope, but hope is never gone, if you're trusting in Me.

When you think that I'm not hearing your prayers, when I seem far away and silent, know that I'm wanting you to seek Me more and learn to trust Me in bigger ways. And remember: There is nothing I can't do.

Lord God, thank You for never leaving
me alone and always helping me to have
faith when life is hard. Amen.

Believe More

"Do not be afraid. Stand firm and you will see
the deliverance the LORD will bring you today."
EXODUS 14:13 (NIV)

There's something you should know—I can do anything.
I have all the power. You don't need to be afraid, I AM
always with you. It might seem like you're all alone, or
like no one cares, but there is no one that cares more
than I do and no one loves you like I do.

Don't get all upset about all of the problems in your
life. Sometimes I allow bad things because they lead to
good things. And sometimes the hard things just give
you the chance to believe in Me more.

Lord, I am thankful that You are always with
me to help me fight my battles. Help me to
not be afraid and to just believe. Amen.

Everything Is Possible

"Everything is possible with God."
MARK 10:27

I see you where you are, but I also see where you are going. You might feel stuck, like the things in your life are just too hard, but nothing is too hard for Me and everything is possible when you're trusting in Me.

Don't lose hope when things seem impossible. Don't be afraid when things don't seem to be going right. Remember that I AM always in control and you can put your hope in Me, I can do anything and everything.

Dear God, sometimes I feel stuck and I need to know
that You will help me. Fill me with hope so that I
can rest knowing that You can do anything. Amen.

Get Up Again

"Get up! For the LORD has given you victory."
JUDGES 7:15

I know you sometimes feel sad and like there is no hope or help for the problems in your life, but I AM your hope and I AM always with you to help you.

Sometimes you will just need to make the decision to believe in Me and choose to hope even when it seems like nothing is going right and things aren't changing. There are times when you are just going to have to get up and choose to believe and choose to have joy because you know that I AM with you.

Lord, help me to be sure of what I believe
and to know that I can trust You to help
me and I can have hope. Amen.

Grow Strong

No unbelief made Abraham waver
concerning the promise of God, but he grew
strong in his faith as he gave glory to God.
ROMANS 4:20 (ESV)

I want you to grow strong in your faith and sometimes that will mean that you must go through hard things. It's the same as how your muscles grow, by using them more and more.

So, instead of seeing troubles in life as bad things, see them as ways to grow in your faith. Look at hard times as opportunities to believe in Me more and a chance to see miracles. So, don't try to always figure things out, all you need to do is keep looking to Me and trusting Me and your faith will grow stronger.

Heavenly Father, I want to be strong in my faith
even when I have to go through hard things.
Help me to see the hard times in my life as
a chance to grow closer to You. Amen.

Wait for Me

Wait for the LORD; be strong and
take heart and wait for the LORD.
PSALM 27:14 (NIV)

There will be lots of times in life when you feel "stuck",
but I will always help you get "unstuck".

I know it's really hard when you pray and nothing
seems to happen. But I want you to remember all of the
promises I've made you and that I always, always keep
My promises.

When your prayers are not answered right away, I
want you to keep praying and just wait … sometimes
amazing things are about to happen.

Lord God, help me to be strong and wait
for You, knowing that when I pray to You,
You will always answer me. Amen.

Wait Quietly

I wait quietly before God, for my victory comes from Him.
PSALM 62:1

When you're worrying, you're not fully trusting in Me. I want you to pray and be sure that I will answer your prayers. I always hear you and I will always help you.

Don't try to make things happen on your own. I AM the One who knows everything and can make the best plans for your life. So, don't worry so much, just enjoy your life and know that I will rescue you, take care of you and give you all you need ... but wait quietly. Don't worry ... things are going to change.

Dear God, help me to wait patiently for
You to answer my prayers. Help me not
to worry and just trust You. Amen.

My Help

We do not know what to do,
but we are looking to You for help.
2 CHRONICLES 20:12

Sometimes, when you are having a hard time in life, you need to realize that you can't always fix things. You need Me and you need My help.

I know that things seem hopeless, like nothing is going to change and everything is getting worse instead of better, but I can do anything. I can do miracles. And I like to surprise you. So, keep asking for My help and keep looking for My surprises.

Lord, I need You and I need Your help. I sometimes feel like there is no hope. Fill me with faith to keep praying and keep looking to You. Amen.

I Will Answer

My times are in Your hands; deliver me from
the hands of my enemies, from those who pursue me.
PSALM 31:15 (NIV)

I don't want you to try so hard to figure things out. The way that I do things can be confusing because I see things differently than you do. I'm God and you're not.

That's why I've given you the Bible, My promises, so that you can have hope and trust Me to do what I promise, when I promise to do it. My timing for answering your prayers is perfect, so just trust Me.

Heavenly Father, help me to trust that
Your timing for answering my prayers is perfect
and that You know what is best for me. Amen.

Keep Hoping

We wait [expectantly] for the Lord; He is our help and
our shield. For in Him our heart rejoices, because we trust
[lean on, rely on, and are confident] in His holy name.
PSALM 33:20-21 (AMP)

When you're stuck, it might seem like there is no hope.
But there is always hope if you're praying to Me and looking to Me for help.

I will always take care of you, but sometimes I will
allow you to go through tough times so that you can
learn that you need Me. You aren't meant to live your life
without Me and without My help. So, when you're stuck,
don't lose hope. Look to Me and I will save you.

Lord, when life gets hard and nothing is changing,
I feel stuck. Please help me to remember that You
will always help me and I can count on You. Amen.

Don't Stay Angry

Therefore each of you must put off falsehood
and speak truthfully to your neighbor,
for we are all members of one body.
EPHESIANS 4:25 (NIV)

There will always be things in your life that will make you angry. And sometimes being angry can make you sin and do wrong things. So, when you're angry, I need you to stop and pray so that I can help you with your anger.

I can help you see things differently and know that everything is going to be okay because I AM in control. So, know that I AM here to help you ... even when you're angry and upset.

Lord, help me to be truthful and speak kindly
of others even when I'm upset and angry. Amen.

I'll Calm You

Don't be quick to get angry,
because anger is typical of fools.
ECCLESIASTES 7:9 (GW)

Even though you might get angry sometimes, you should not be angry all the time. My Spirit within you will help you to be patient, loving and peaceful.

It's okay to feel angry. Anger can make you want to help others who are treated badly or be kind to someone who needs a friend. But I want you to rely on Me to help you calm your anger so that it does not control you in a bad way. I don't want anger to steal your joy.

Dear God, sometimes I get angry and
I lose my peace. Please help me to have
a quiet heart that is calm and joyful. Amen.

Calm in the Storm

A hot-tempered man stirs up strife, but he who
is slow to anger and patient calms disputes.
PROVERBS 15:18 (AMP)

I don't want you looking for reasons to be angry. There
are enough problems in life ... I don't want you to be
angry about everything all of the time.

The heart and mind I've given you is peaceful, patient, and loving. And even though sometimes you might
experience the feeling of anger, I want you to learn to let
go of your anger so it doesn't keep you from having the
joyful life you're supposed to have.

Lord God, I get angry and want to get
back at those who upset me. Help me to
be peaceful and let things go. Amen.

Don't Be Angry

But now is the time to get rid of anger, rage,
malicious behavior, slander, and dirty language.
Don't lie to each other, for you have stripped off
your old sinful nature and all its wicked deeds.

COLOSSIANS 3:8-9

There are some things in your life that you just need to get rid of. I know things and people can make you angry, but it ends up hurting you more than them.

I want you to come to Me when you're angry or someone has hurt you. I will help you to have peace instead of feeling anger and wanting revenge. I don't want you to try and get back at others and hurt them because they hurt you. I want you to trust Me to handle it all.

Heavenly Father, help me to release my anger
to You. Give me the strength to love others
instead of hating when I am hurt. Amen.

Treat Others Well

"Do to others as you would like them to do to you."
LUKE 6:31

I know that sometimes others can be mean and hurt your feelings. But I don't want you to hurt them back. I want you to show them that you are Mine, that you have My heart and then maybe they will believe in Me too.

You should always treat others the way you want them to treat you. Don't allow anger or jealousy to steal your joy. Even when others are mean to you, just be nice to them.

Lord God, when others hurt me,
help me to still be kind to them and
come to You to heal my heart. Amen.

My Grace Is Free

By grace you have been saved through faith.
And this is not your own doing; it is the gift of God.
EPHESIANS 2:8 (ESV)

Because I love you, I've given you hope through My grace, and it's free! There's nothing you can do to earn my grace or lose it. So don't get down when life doesn't go right, or you get in trouble, I will always help you when you come to Me.

So, don't think that you have to do everything right. Even when you make mistakes, I will forgive you. Just know that no matter what, I love you and nothing can take away My love for you.

Lord God, thank You for Your grace, so that even when I get in trouble, I can come to You without fear and know that You will love me and help me. Amen.

Accept My Grace

He said, "My grace is all you need. My power
works best in weakness." So now I am glad
to boast about my weaknesses, so that the
power of Christ can work through me.
2 CORINTHIANS 12:9

Sometimes you think you need lots of things, but actually
you just need Me and the grace I give you. Know that
when life is really hard, I'm giving you the chance to get
closer to Me, to count on Me, to learn to trust Me.

It's a way that you can grow stronger in your faith and
realize that you really can trust Me. All you really need is
Me—it's My grace and love that will get you through any
situation. Just keep believing and trusting.

Heavenly Father, I am so thankful for
Your grace because I mess up and I need
to be forgiven. Thank You for Your love
that will get me through anything. Amen.

Stop Worrying

Those who trust in the L ᴏʀᴅ will lack no good thing.

PSALM 34:10

I never want you to worry. I know sometimes it's hard, but you really don't need to worry because I'm always in control. There is nothing I can't do and My love for you never changes.

I want you to be sure, because I've promised you that I will always take care of you. Even if it seems like things aren't going right, you can be sure that I AM working to make all things in your life work out well.

Lord God, thank You for all of the
good things in my life. I know they come
from You and Your love for me. Amen.

Still Your Fear

Do not be anxious about anything.
PHILIPPIANS 4:6 (NIV)

I want you to be sure that you can trust Me. I've made you promises and I do not lie. I know everything, and I have all the power. I watch over you—day and night— when you're awake and when you're sleeping. There is nothing at all for you to fear. You do not have to worry when you're trusting in Me.

So, when you feel like life is falling apart, know that if you trust Me, I will take care of everything. Seek Me first and you'll have all that you need.

Heavenly Father, sometimes I feel like
things are falling apart and I need to know
that You keep Your promises and I'll have
all I need. Please guide me. Amen.

You're Never Alone

It is not that we think we are qualified to do anything
on our own. Our qualification comes from God.
2 CORINTHIANS 3:5

You need to know that I will always be with you and I will always take care of everything that is important in your life. There will always be hard times, there will always be things that just don't go right, but you can trust Me to work it all out.

I just want you to learn to be strong, to have faith and keep believing—no matter what. I can work miracles, so you should never give up. There is nothing that is too hard for Me.

Lord, help me to be strong and have
faith and realize that I cannot do
everything on my own ... I need You. Amen.

Stay at My Feet

Exalt the LORD our God
and worship at His footstool; He is holy.
PSALM 99:5 (NIV)

When you worship Me, praising Me for who I AM—your God—your Savior—I see your faith. If you totally trust Me, if you focus on Me instead of your problems, you'll find yourself at My feet.

I want you to let go of trying to be in control of your life. Only I can do what you can't—only I can do the impossible. And it's when you're focused on Me, praising and worshiping Me, that miracles happen.

Lord, I am so thankful for who You are …
for Your love and Your forgiveness, for Your
grace that always saves me. Amen.

Nothing Is Too Hard

"O Sovereign LORD! You made the heavens and
earth by Your strong hand and powerful arm.
Nothing is too hard for You!"
JEREMIAH 32:17

I know that sometimes you're worried that your troubles
are too hard and I can't answer your prayers, but you
need to know that NOTHING is too hard for Me.

I want you to see Me as being bigger than all of the
problems in your life. And then I want you to trust Me to
do what is best. Know that I will never fail you and then
trust that I can do the miracles you need Me to.

Lord God, help me to know that You can do
anything and nothing is too difficult or impossible
for You, even when things seem hopeless. Amen.

Power in Praise

Paul and Silas were praying and singing hymns
of praise to God. Suddenly, a violent earthquake
shook the foundations of the jail. All the doors flew
open, and all the prisoners' chains came loose.
ACTS 16:25-26 (GW)

When you feel like things are bad and just getting worse, when the only thing that can change things is a miracle, know that I will help you and there is power in your praise.

When you praise Me and thank Me for all I've done and all I'm yet to do, know that I hear your faith and My power will be released from heaven. And even when life is hard, I want you to praise Me, it shows what you expect Me to do—to help you, to save you, to give you hope.

Heavenly Father, help me to praise You,
expecting Your power in my life.
Give me hope when I have none. Amen.

Prayers of Praise

It is good to give thanks to the LORD,
to sing praises to the Most High.

PSALM 92:1

When you pray to Me, I want you to pray to Me full of praise and filled with hope. You may not feel like there is anything in your life to be praising Me for, but you can't see and know all that I do.

I AM in control of all that concerns you. Even though you can't always see what I'm doing, I AM always at work, always making all things work together for good. There is nothing for you to fear. Just give thanks and pray with praise.

Lord God, I pray to You full of praises.
My heart is filled with hope because my hope
is in You and I know that You have promised
to turn all things together for good. Amen.

The Time Is Now

"The time is coming—indeed it's here now—
when true worshipers will worship the Father
in spirit and in truth. The Father is looking for
those who will worship Him that way."

JOHN 4:23

There may never seem to be a right time to pray, but every moment of your life you should be praying and when you come to Me in prayer, I want you to be full of hope and praise.

I want you to come into My presence, ready to hear My voice as I speak to your heart. I want you to trust Me ... that even though nothing seems to be going right, I AM working to keep My promises to you. So, call on Me, believe in Me, the time to pray and hope is right now.

God, help me praise You every second
of every day in prayer. Open my heart
and let me hear Your voice. Amen.